Coastal Resilience Through Nature-Based Solutions: Strategies for Ecosystem Restoration and Climate Adaptation

Copyright

Coastal Resilience Through Nature-Based Solutions: Strategies for Ecosystem Restoration and Climate Adaptation

© 2025 Robert C. Brears

Published by **Global Climate Solutions**

ISBN (eBook): 978-1-991369-17-8

ISBN (Paperback): 978-1-991369-18-5

Table of Contents

Preface

Introduction: A Blueprint for Coastal Restoration Through Nature-Based Solutions

Chapter 1: Mangroves as Coastal Buffers

Chapter 2: Coral Reef Restoration and Conservation

Chapter 3: Seagrass Meadows for Marine Biodiversity

Chapter 4: Salt Marshes for Flood Mitigation

Chapter 5: Wetlands for Coastal Resilience

Chapter 6: Dunes and Beaches for Erosion Control

Chapter 7: Living Shorelines for Coastal Adaptation

Chapter 8: Oyster and Shellfish Reefs for Coastal Restoration

Chapter 9: Urban NbS for Coastal Cities

Chapter 10: Scaling Up NbS for Global Coastal Restoration

Conclusion

Preface

Coasts are dynamic landscapes where land meets the ocean, shaping ecosystems that support biodiversity, provide livelihoods, and act as natural defenses against storms and rising seas. Yet, in an era of climate uncertainty, these fragile environments face mounting threats. Rising sea levels, extreme weather events, habitat destruction, and human-induced pressures are accelerating the degradation of coastal ecosystems, placing both nature and human communities at risk.

As the world grapples with these challenges, Nature-Based Solutions (NbS) have emerged as a promising way forward. By restoring, protecting, and enhancing coastal ecosystems, NbS provide a sustainable alternative to traditional engineering approaches. They harness the power of natural processes—mangroves dissipating wave energy, coral reefs buffering shorelines, wetlands absorbing floodwaters—to strengthen coastal resilience in ways that benefit both people and the environment.

This book explores the transformative potential of NbS in safeguarding coasts against climate change. Through an in-depth examination of diverse ecosystems—from mangrove forests and seagrass meadows to oyster reefs and living shorelines—it highlights the strategies, benefits, and challenges of implementing NbS at scale. In doing so, it makes the case for rethinking coastal adaptation, shifting from reactive, hard infrastructure solutions to proactive, nature-driven resilience.

Coastal ecosystems are not just landscapes; they are lifelines. Their preservation is not merely an environmental concern—it is a necessity for securing a livable future for coastal communities worldwide. By embracing NbS, we can move toward a vision where nature is not only protected but also restored as a cornerstone of climate adaptation. This book serves as a guide to that vision, offering insights into how coastal resilience can be built through nature.

Introduction: A Blueprint for Coastal Restoration Through Nature-Based Solutions

Coastal ecosystems are among the most dynamic and vital environments on Earth, acting as buffers against storms, habitats for biodiversity, and sources of livelihoods for millions of people. Yet, these ecosystems are increasingly under threat. Climate change, rising sea levels, pollution, and human activity have significantly degraded coastal habitats, undermining their ability to sustain both ecological and economic systems.

Amidst these challenges, Nature-Based Solutions (NbS) offer a powerful approach to restoring and conserving coastal ecosystems. By leveraging natural processes and ecosystems, NbS not only address environmental issues but also provide sustainable, cost-effective, and resilient alternatives to traditional infrastructure. From mangrove reforestation to coral reef restoration, these solutions hold the potential to safeguard coastal areas while promoting biodiversity and climate adaptation.

This introduction sets the stage for exploring how NbS can transform coastal conservation efforts. It outlines the urgent need for action, the global significance of coastal ecosystems, and the principles guiding NbS implementation. As the book unfolds, it will delve into specific types of NbS, showcasing their potential to restore, conserve, and future-proof our coasts in an era of uncertainty.

Definition and Importance of Nature-Based Solutions for Coastal Restoration

NbS are a framework of strategies that utilize natural processes and ecosystems to address societal challenges, including those related to climate change, disaster risk reduction, biodiversity loss, and sustainable development. In the context of coastal restoration, NbS involve interventions that conserve, restore, or enhance coastal ecosystems, such as mangroves, coral reefs, salt marshes, and seagrass meadows, while simultaneously delivering benefits to human communities. These solutions prioritize working with nature rather than against it, blending ecological knowledge with sustainable management practices.

The importance of NbS for coastal restoration lies in their ability to address critical environmental challenges while promoting resilience and sustainability. Coastal ecosystems play a vital role in protecting shorelines, absorbing carbon dioxide, and providing habitats for marine and terrestrial species. However, decades of habitat destruction, pollution, and overexploitation have degraded these ecosystems, making them more vulnerable to the impacts of climate change, including rising sea levels, increased storm intensity, and coastal erosion. Traditional approaches to coastal protection, such as seawalls and breakwaters, often fail to account for the dynamic and interconnected nature of ecosystems, leading to unintended environmental consequences and escalating costs over time.

NbS offer a compelling alternative by combining ecological restoration with societal benefits. For example, restoring mangrove forests can reduce the impact of storm surges, protect coastal communities from flooding, and create critical habitats for fish and other species that support local livelihoods. Similarly, rehabilitating coral reefs can enhance biodiversity, support tourism, and buffer coastlines against wave energy. These solutions are inherently adaptive, evolving with changing environmental conditions, unlike rigid, engineered structures that may require costly repairs or replacements.

Another key advantage of NbS is their capacity to deliver multiple co-benefits. Beyond environmental protection, they contribute to carbon sequestration, improving water quality, and fostering economic opportunities, such as ecotourism and sustainable fisheries. Moreover, they often align with global frameworks, such as the United Nations Sustainable Development Goals (SDGs) and the Paris Agreement, making them an integral part of international efforts to combat climate change and biodiversity loss.

Implementing NbS for coastal restoration also emphasizes community involvement and inclusive decision-making. Local knowledge and participation are critical for designing effective and sustainable interventions, ensuring that restoration efforts address the needs and priorities of those most affected by environmental degradation. Empowering communities not only fosters stewardship but also strengthens social resilience, creating a collective capacity to respond to future challenges.

As the world faces mounting environmental pressures, the urgency to adopt NbS for coastal restoration has never been greater. These solutions represent a paradigm shift, moving away from reactive, short-term fixes toward proactive, holistic approaches that integrate ecological, social, and economic dimensions. By embracing NbS, coastal regions can safeguard their ecosystems, protect human livelihoods, and build resilience against an uncertain future.

Overview of Challenges to Coastal Ecosystems

Coastal ecosystems, encompassing mangroves, coral reefs, seagrass meadows, salt marshes, and wetlands, are critical to the health of the planet and the well-being of human communities. These ecosystems provide essential services, including coastal protection, carbon sequestration, water filtration, and habitat provision for diverse species. Despite their importance, coastal ecosystems are under increasing pressure from a combination of natural and human-induced challenges.

One of the most significant threats to coastal ecosystems is climate change. Rising global temperatures have caused sea levels to increase due to the melting of polar ice caps and the thermal expansion of seawater. This phenomenon leads to the inundation of low-lying coastal areas, erodes shorelines, and destroys habitats such as mangroves and salt marshes. Additionally, climate change intensifies the frequency and severity of extreme weather events, such as hurricanes, typhoons, and storm surges. These events result in significant damage to coastal environments, uprooting vegetation, eroding dunes, and degrading coral reefs.

Ocean warming, another consequence of climate change, poses a direct threat to coral reefs. Warmer sea temperatures cause coral bleaching, a stress response where corals expel the symbiotic algae that provide them with energy. Without these algae, corals are unable to survive, leading to widespread reef degradation. Ocean acidification, caused by the absorption of excess atmospheric carbon dioxide into the oceans, further exacerbates the decline of coral reefs and shellfish populations by weakening their calcium carbonate structures.

Human activities, such as urbanization and coastal development, also contribute to the degradation of coastal ecosystems. Expanding cities, resorts, and ports often require the clearing of mangroves, wetlands, and other habitats to make way for infrastructure. These activities disrupt natural processes, reduce biodiversity, and expose coastlines to increased erosion and flooding. In addition, land reclamation and dredging operations can disturb sediment balances, causing further harm to marine ecosystems.

Pollution is another pervasive challenge. Coastal areas often serve as the final destination for agricultural runoff, industrial discharges, and untreated wastewater. Excessive nutrients from fertilizers lead to eutrophication, a process that depletes oxygen levels in the water and creates "dead zones" where aquatic life cannot survive. Plastics and other forms of marine debris accumulate in coastal waters, entangling marine organisms and disrupting their habitats. Oil spills and chemical contaminants also pose long-lasting threats, particularly to sensitive ecosystems like mangroves and seagrass meadows.

Overexploitation of natural resources has further strained coastal ecosystems. Unsustainable fishing practices, such as trawling and dynamite fishing, destroy habitats and deplete fish stocks. Harvesting of mangrove wood for fuel and construction weakens these ecosystems' ability to provide critical services. In many regions, tourism-driven demand for seafood and coastal attractions exacerbates resource extraction, placing additional pressure on already fragile ecosystems.

Invasive species, often introduced through ballast water from ships or aquaculture operations, pose another threat to coastal ecosystems. These non-native organisms can outcompete native species, disrupt food webs, and alter ecosystem dynamics. For example, invasive plants can overtake salt marshes, reducing their capacity to filter water and provide habitat for native species. Similarly, invasive predators can decimate populations of native fish and invertebrates.

Fragmented governance and inadequate enforcement of environmental regulations compound the challenges faced by coastal ecosystems. In many regions, coastal management is hindered by overlapping jurisdictions, competing interests, and insufficient funding. This lack of coordination leads to unregulated development, weak pollution controls, and limited restoration efforts. Furthermore, the voices of local communities, who are often the most affected by ecosystem degradation, are frequently excluded from decision-making processes.

The cumulative impact of these challenges threatens the resilience of coastal ecosystems and the services they provide. Degraded habitats are less capable of withstanding and recovering from environmental stressors, making them more vulnerable to future impacts. The loss of biodiversity, in turn, reduces the ecological functions that underpin these ecosystems, such as nutrient cycling, sediment stabilization, and primary production.

Addressing these challenges requires a comprehensive and integrated approach that combines scientific knowledge, community involvement, and policy support. NbS offer a promising path forward, leveraging the inherent resilience of ecosystems to tackle environmental issues while delivering benefits to society. By understanding the threats faced by coastal ecosystems, we can better design and implement strategies to conserve and restore them, ensuring their sustainability for future generations.

Objectives and Structure of the Book

The degradation of coastal ecosystems has reached critical levels, driven by climate change, unsustainable development, and resource exploitation. These ecosystems are vital for the health of our planet, offering services such as coastal protection, carbon sequestration, and habitat provision for countless species. Recognizing the urgency to act, this book aims to provide a comprehensive exploration of NbS as an effective approach for conserving and restoring coastal ecosystems.

The primary objective of this book is to highlight the potential of NbS in addressing the challenges facing coastal environments. It seeks to inform readers about the diverse types of NbS that can be employed to enhance the resilience of coastal ecosystems while delivering significant environmental, economic, and social benefits. By focusing on specific types of solutions, such as mangrove reforestation, coral reef restoration, and wetland conservation, the book provides a detailed understanding of how each approach contributes to ecosystem restoration and long-term sustainability.

Another key goal of this book is to bridge the gap between theory and practice. While NbS are increasingly recognized for their effectiveness, their implementation requires careful planning, scientific knowledge, and stakeholder involvement. This book offers insights into the ecological principles underlying NbS, the techniques used in their application, and the challenges that need to be addressed to ensure success. By doing so, it equips readers with the knowledge needed to design and implement effective restoration strategies.

The book also emphasizes the importance of integrating NbS into broader coastal management and climate adaptation frameworks. Coastal ecosystems do not exist in isolation; they are interconnected with adjacent ecosystems, human communities, and economic activities. Effective restoration efforts must consider these interconnections, ensuring that NbS are part of holistic approaches that address multiple objectives, such as disaster risk reduction, biodiversity conservation, and sustainable livelihoods.

The structure of this book is designed to guide readers through a logical progression, starting with foundational knowledge and advancing to specific applications and future directions. The introduction sets the stage by defining NbS, explaining their relevance to coastal restoration, and outlining the key challenges facing coastal ecosystems. It provides a context for understanding why NbS are a critical tool for addressing these challenges.

The book is organized into ten chapters, each focusing on a specific type of NbS. These chapters delve into the ecological functions, restoration techniques, and practical applications of various solutions, such as mangroves, coral reefs, seagrass meadows, salt marshes, and wetlands. By dedicating a chapter to each solution, the book ensures a detailed exploration of their unique contributions to coastal resilience and biodiversity.

In addition to examining natural ecosystems, the book includes chapters on innovative approaches, such as living shorelines and urban NbS. Living shorelines blend natural elements with engineered solutions, offering a sustainable alternative to traditional hard infrastructure. Urban NbS focus on incorporating natural processes into city planning, addressing challenges such as stormwater management and urban heat islands while enhancing the resilience of coastal cities.

The final chapter discusses strategies for scaling up NbS at regional and global levels. It highlights the importance of cross-sectoral collaboration, community involvement, and supportive policy frameworks in achieving widespread adoption of NbS. The chapter also explores emerging trends and technologies, such as remote sensing and artificial intelligence, that can enhance the effectiveness and efficiency of NbS implementation.

Throughout the book, the emphasis is on providing readers with actionable knowledge and practical insights. While the focus remains on the ecological aspects of NbS, the discussion also considers socio-economic and governance dimensions. This holistic perspective ensures that the book addresses the complexity of coastal restoration, offering solutions that are not only scientifically sound but also socially inclusive and economically viable.

The intended audience for this book includes environmental professionals, researchers, policymakers, and students interested in coastal conservation and restoration. By presenting a clear and concise overview of NbS, supported by scientific principles and practical examples, the book aims to inspire and empower its readers to take meaningful action in preserving coastal ecosystems.

In summary, this book seeks to achieve three key objectives:

1. To provide a comprehensive understanding of the role and potential of NbS in conserving and restoring coastal ecosystems.

2. To equip readers with the knowledge and tools needed to design and implement effective restoration strategies.

3. To promote the integration of NbS into broader coastal management and climate adaptation frameworks.

The structure of the book reflects these objectives, guiding readers from foundational knowledge to specific applications and future directions. By focusing on the diverse types of NbS and their contributions to coastal resilience, this book aims to serve as a valuable resource for anyone committed to the sustainability of our planet's coasts.

Chapter 1: Mangroves as Coastal Buffers

This chapter delves into the ecological and protective functions of mangroves, highlighting their importance in coastal resilience and climate adaptation. It explores the techniques used for their restoration, including reforestation and hydrological interventions, and addresses the challenges associated with maintaining these ecosystems. By understanding the role of mangroves as coastal buffers, we can appreciate their value in building sustainable and adaptive coastal systems.

Role of Mangroves in Coastal Protection and Biodiversity

Mangroves are unique coastal ecosystems located at the intersection of land and sea, where they provide a range of ecological, social, and economic benefits. These salt-tolerant forests are predominantly found in tropical and subtropical regions, where their dense root systems and foliage make them vital components of coastal environments. Among their most critical functions are coastal protection and biodiversity support, both of which play a significant role in maintaining the resilience of coastal ecosystems and communities.

One of the primary roles of mangroves is protecting coastlines from natural hazards. The intricate root systems of mangroves stabilize sediment, reducing coastal erosion and preventing land loss. These roots trap sediments that would otherwise be washed away by waves and tides, allowing coastal areas to retain their structure even during periods of high wave activity. Additionally, the above-ground roots dissipate wave energy, reducing the impact of storm surges and high tides on coastal areas. This function is particularly important in regions prone to cyclones, hurricanes, and tsunamis, as mangroves can act as a natural buffer, protecting human settlements and infrastructure from catastrophic damage.

In the context of climate change, mangroves are crucial in mitigating the impacts of rising sea levels. Their ability to trap sediments helps coastal areas keep pace with sea-level rise, providing a natural mechanism for maintaining land elevation. Moreover, mangroves play a significant role in protecting freshwater systems from saltwater intrusion, preserving the water resources necessary for agriculture, drinking water, and ecosystem health. The presence of mangroves along coastlines can significantly reduce the economic costs associated with repairing and replacing man-made infrastructure damaged by flooding and erosion.

In addition to their protective functions, mangroves are biodiversity hotspots that support a wide range of terrestrial and marine species. They provide critical habitats for numerous organisms, including fish, crabs, shrimp, and mollusks, many of which rely on mangroves for spawning, nursery, and feeding grounds. The structural complexity of mangrove forests, with their interwoven roots and canopies, creates a safe haven for juvenile marine species, helping sustain fisheries that are vital for food security and local economies. In this way, mangroves contribute to the health of adjacent ecosystems, such as coral reefs and seagrass meadows, which are interconnected through nutrient and energy flows.

The biodiversity within mangrove forests is not limited to marine life. They also serve as habitats for a variety of terrestrial species, including birds, reptiles, and mammals. Many migratory bird species rely on mangroves as resting and feeding sites during their journeys. Additionally, mangroves support endangered and endemic species, playing a critical role in global biodiversity conservation efforts. The loss of mangroves would have cascading effects on these species, leading to declines in populations and disruptions to ecological processes.

Mangroves also play a key role in carbon sequestration, acting as "blue carbon" ecosystems. They store significant amounts of carbon in their biomass and in the soil beneath them, making them valuable allies in the fight against climate change. The carbon storage capacity of mangroves is far greater per unit area than many terrestrial forests, highlighting their importance in global carbon cycling. Protecting and restoring mangroves is therefore essential for maintaining their role as carbon sinks, reducing greenhouse gas concentrations, and mitigating climate change impacts.

Despite their critical importance, mangroves face numerous threats that jeopardize their ability to provide these ecosystem services. Urbanization, agriculture, and aquaculture have led to widespread deforestation and degradation of mangrove forests. Pollution, including nutrient runoff and plastic waste, further impacts the health of these ecosystems, reducing their capacity to support biodiversity and protect coastlines. Climate change poses additional risks, with rising temperatures and sea levels threatening the survival of mangroves in many regions.

Recognizing the vital role of mangroves in coastal protection and biodiversity is essential for their conservation and restoration. NbS that integrate mangrove restoration into broader coastal management strategies can enhance the resilience of both ecosystems and communities. These solutions not only safeguard the ecological functions of mangroves but also provide long-term economic and social benefits, demonstrating the value of investing in the protection of these critical ecosystems.

Techniques for Mangrove Restoration (Reforestation, Hydrology, Propagule Planting)

Mangrove restoration is a vital process aimed at rehabilitating degraded or lost mangrove forests, ensuring the recovery of their ecological functions and benefits. Successful mangrove restoration requires a comprehensive understanding of the local environment, careful planning, and the implementation of appropriate techniques. This section focuses on three key restoration techniques: reforestation, hydrological restoration, and propagule planting, each of which offers unique benefits and applications depending on site conditions.

Reforestation of Mangroves

Reforestation involves the planting or natural regeneration of mangroves in areas where they have been degraded or lost. It is one of the most widely used techniques for restoring mangrove ecosystems. The process begins with site selection, which involves identifying suitable areas where mangroves once thrived or where conditions support their growth. Factors such as soil salinity, tidal patterns, and elevation are critical in determining whether a site is viable for mangrove reforestation.

The choice of mangrove species is another important consideration. Native species that are well-adapted to local environmental conditions should be prioritized, as they are more likely to thrive and support local biodiversity. For instance, *Rhizophora* species are commonly used in many regions due to their robust root structures and ability to stabilize sediment. In some cases, mixed-species planting is employed to mimic natural diversity and enhance ecosystem resilience.

Reforestation efforts often utilize nursery-grown seedlings, which are cultivated in controlled environments before being transplanted into the restoration site. This approach ensures that the seedlings are healthy and well-established, increasing their chances of survival in challenging environments. Planting is typically carried out in alignment with tidal patterns to optimize water availability and nutrient uptake.

One of the challenges of mangrove reforestation is the risk of failure due to unsuitable site conditions or lack of community involvement. Engaging local communities in the planning and implementation process can significantly improve outcomes by fostering stewardship and ensuring long-term monitoring and maintenance.

Hydrological Restoration

Hydrological restoration focuses on restoring the natural water flow and tidal patterns necessary for mangrove growth and survival. Many degraded mangrove areas have been affected by changes in hydrology due to infrastructure development, such as roads, dams, and aquaculture ponds, which block tidal inflows and disrupt sediment and nutrient cycles.

The first step in hydrological restoration is identifying the specific alterations that have impacted the site's water flow. This involves conducting detailed hydrological assessments, including mapping tidal channels, measuring salinity levels, and understanding sediment deposition patterns. Once the disruptions are understood, interventions can be designed to restore the natural tidal regime.

Common interventions include the removal of physical barriers, such as embankments or dikes, to allow tidal waters to flow freely into the restoration site. In cases where removing barriers is not feasible, culverts or sluice gates can be installed to regulate water flow. These structures ensure that tidal waters reach the mangrove area while preventing excessive flooding.

Another aspect of hydrological restoration is addressing soil conditions. In degraded sites, soils may become compacted or acidic, limiting the establishment of mangroves. Techniques such as soil aeration, addition of organic matter, or liming to neutralize acidity can help improve soil conditions and support mangrove growth.

Hydrological restoration is often combined with other techniques, such as natural regeneration or propagule planting, to maximize the success of restoration efforts. By addressing the underlying hydrological issues, this approach creates conditions that allow mangroves to reestablish naturally over time.

Propagule Planting

Propagule planting is a direct and widely used method for mangrove restoration, involving the collection and planting of propagules—

seedlings or seeds that develop while still attached to the parent tree. This technique is particularly effective in areas where natural regeneration is limited due to seed dispersal barriers or high levels of disturbance.

The process begins with the collection of propagules from healthy mangrove forests. Timing is crucial, as propagules must be collected during their optimal maturation stage to ensure viability. Once collected, the propagules are transported to the restoration site, where they are planted directly into the soil.

Planting density is an important consideration in propagule planting. Dense planting may initially provide better erosion control and higher survival rates, but overcrowding can lead to competition for light and nutrients as the trees grow. Conversely, sparse planting may leave the area vulnerable to erosion and limit the ecosystem's ability to recover. Balancing these factors is essential for achieving long-term restoration success.

Another key factor in propagule planting is site preparation. In areas with strong wave action or unstable soils, measures such as the installation of wave barriers or the use of biodegradable planting pods may be necessary to protect propagules from being washed away. In some cases, artificial structures like bamboo fences or coir logs are used to create sheltered microenvironments that enhance propagule establishment.

Monitoring and maintenance are critical to the success of propagule planting. Regular inspections help identify issues such as herbivory, disease, or poor survival rates. Where necessary, replanting or additional interventions can be carried out to address these challenges and improve outcomes.

Integration of Techniques

In practice, mangrove restoration often involves a combination of these techniques to address the specific needs of the restoration site.

For example, hydrological restoration may be carried out first to create suitable conditions for reforestation or propagule planting. Similarly, propagule planting may be used to supplement natural regeneration in areas where seed dispersal is limited.

Challenges and Future Considerations in Mangrove Restoration

Mangrove restoration holds immense potential for enhancing coastal resilience, supporting biodiversity, and mitigating climate change. However, the implementation of restoration projects is not without challenges. These obstacles range from technical and ecological limitations to socio-economic and governance issues. Addressing these challenges is critical for ensuring the long-term success and sustainability of restoration efforts. Additionally, future considerations must incorporate adaptive strategies, innovative approaches, and inclusive frameworks to maximize the benefits of mangrove restoration in a rapidly changing world.

Challenges in Mangrove Restoration

One of the primary challenges in mangrove restoration is the complexity of site selection. Mangroves require specific environmental conditions, including suitable tidal ranges, salinity levels, and sediment types. Restoration projects often fail because sites are chosen based on availability rather than ecological suitability. For instance, planting mangroves in areas that do not naturally support them, such as high-energy sandy beaches, can lead to low survival rates and wasted resources.

Hydrological disruption poses another significant obstacle. Many degraded mangrove areas suffer from altered water flow caused by infrastructure development, such as roads, dikes, and aquaculture ponds. These disruptions prevent tidal waters from reaching mangrove habitats, depriving them of essential nutrients and sediments. Restoring natural hydrology is a complex and resource-intensive process that requires extensive planning and collaboration among stakeholders.

Climate change exacerbates these challenges, introducing new variables that complicate restoration efforts. Rising sea levels can submerge restoration sites, particularly in low-lying areas where sediment accumulation cannot keep pace with water level increases. Ocean warming and acidification also threaten mangrove health, affecting their ability to regenerate and sustain biodiversity. These factors highlight the need for restoration projects to account for long-term climate impacts.

Another critical challenge is the prevalence of monoculture planting in restoration projects. Many initiatives focus on a single mangrove species, such as *Rhizophora*, due to its ease of planting and initial survival rates. However, monocultures are less resilient to environmental stressors and do not support the same level of biodiversity as mixed-species forests. This practice limits the ecological functions of restored mangroves and increases the risk of failure.

Socio-economic factors also play a significant role in the success or failure of mangrove restoration projects. Conflicting land-use priorities, such as agriculture, aquaculture, and urban development, often compete with restoration efforts. Local communities, who rely on mangrove areas for resources like firewood and fish, may resist restoration if they perceive it as limiting their livelihoods. Inadequate community involvement in the planning and implementation phases can lead to a lack of local support, reducing the likelihood of long-term success.

Governance and funding are additional barriers to effective mangrove restoration. In many regions, fragmented governance structures and unclear land tenure rights complicate project coordination. Limited financial resources often restrict the scale of restoration efforts, and short-term funding cycles fail to support the long-term monitoring and maintenance required for successful restoration. Without stable and consistent investment, restoration projects risk stagnating or failing to achieve their objectives.

Future Considerations in Mangrove Restoration

To overcome these challenges, future mangrove restoration efforts must adopt a more integrated and adaptive approach. One key consideration is the use of science-based methodologies for site selection. Advanced technologies such as remote sensing, GIS mapping, and hydrological modeling can help identify suitable restoration sites with high potential for success. Incorporating these tools into the planning process ensures that projects are designed with a solid ecological foundation.

Enhancing species diversity in restoration projects is another critical consideration. Mixed-species planting not only improves ecosystem resilience but also supports a wider range of biodiversity and ecological functions. Future initiatives should prioritize the use of native species that reflect the natural composition of the region, ensuring that restored forests closely resemble their original state.

Community involvement is essential for the long-term success of mangrove restoration. Engaging local stakeholders in every stage of the process—from planning and implementation to monitoring and maintenance—fosters a sense of ownership and stewardship. Education and capacity-building programs can help communities understand the benefits of mangrove restoration and actively participate in its success. Co-management frameworks, where local communities and governments share responsibilities, can further strengthen these efforts.

Climate adaptation strategies must also be central to future restoration efforts. Restoration plans should incorporate projections of sea-level rise, temperature changes, and storm intensity to ensure long-term viability. Techniques such as sediment augmentation and the creation of buffer zones can help mangroves adapt to changing conditions. Additionally, integrating mangrove restoration into broader coastal management and climate resilience frameworks ensures that these efforts contribute to wider environmental and societal goals.

Innovative financing mechanisms can address funding challenges and ensure the sustainability of restoration projects. Payments for ecosystem services (PES), carbon offset programs, and public-private partnerships offer opportunities to generate long-term financial support. Governments, non-governmental organizations, and businesses can collaborate to create funding models that align restoration efforts with economic incentives.

Finally, monitoring and evaluation are crucial for ensuring the effectiveness of mangrove restoration. Robust monitoring programs that track ecological, social, and economic outcomes allow practitioners to identify challenges early and adjust strategies as needed. Using standardized metrics and reporting frameworks enhances transparency and facilitates knowledge-sharing among stakeholders.

Chapter 2: Coral Reef Restoration and Conservation

Coral reefs, often referred to as the "rainforests of the sea," are among the most biodiverse ecosystems on the planet. These intricate underwater structures provide critical habitats for marine species, support coastal livelihoods, and offer natural protection against waves and storms. However, coral reefs face unprecedented threats from climate change, pollution, overfishing, and destructive practices, leading to widespread degradation.

This chapter delves into the importance of coral reefs for marine ecosystems and coastal resilience, emphasizing their role as a nature-based solution for addressing coastal challenges. It explores innovative techniques for coral reef restoration, such as coral gardening, micro-fragmentation, and the use of artificial reef structures. Additionally, the chapter examines the challenges of conserving coral reefs in a warming and acidifying ocean, highlighting the need for adaptive strategies and integrated conservation efforts.

By understanding the ecological and societal value of coral reefs, as well as the approaches to their restoration and conservation, this chapter provides a foundation for harnessing their potential in creating sustainable and resilient coastal ecosystems.

Importance of Coral Reefs in Marine Ecosystems

Coral reefs are among the most vital and diverse ecosystems on Earth, often referred to as the "rainforests of the sea" due to their extraordinary biodiversity. Found in tropical and subtropical regions, these ecosystems are built by colonies of coral polyps, which secrete calcium carbonate to form intricate reef structures over time. Despite covering less than 1% of the ocean floor, coral reefs support approximately 25% of all marine species, making them critical to the health and productivity of marine ecosystems.

One of the primary roles of coral reefs is providing habitat and shelter for a vast array of marine organisms. The complex structure of reefs creates numerous niches, offering food, breeding grounds, and protection for species ranging from tiny invertebrates to large predators. Fish, mollusks, crustaceans, and other marine animals depend on coral reefs for their survival, either directly as part of the reef community or indirectly through the food web. This biodiversity contributes to the overall resilience of marine ecosystems, enabling them to withstand and recover from environmental changes.

Coral reefs also play a crucial role in the global marine food web. They serve as primary habitats for many species of fish and other marine organisms that are vital to both aquatic ecosystems and human communities. Many commercially important fish species, such as grouper and snapper, rely on coral reefs during key stages of their life cycles. These species often begin their lives in the protection of the reef before migrating to other marine environments. The health of coral reefs directly influences the productivity of fisheries and the availability of seafood for millions of people worldwide.

Beyond their ecological importance, coral reefs provide significant benefits to coastal environments through their role in coastal protection. Reefs act as natural barriers, dissipating wave energy and reducing the impact of storm surges, hurricanes, and tsunamis on coastal areas. By absorbing up to 97% of wave energy, coral reefs protect shorelines from erosion and flooding, safeguarding both natural habitats and human infrastructure. This protective function is especially crucial for low-lying island nations and coastal communities vulnerable to the impacts of climate change and extreme weather events.

Coral reefs also contribute to global biogeochemical cycles, particularly the carbon and nutrient cycles. Coral organisms capture carbon dioxide from seawater to build their calcium carbonate skeletons, playing a role in regulating atmospheric CO_2 levels. Additionally, the interactions between coral reefs and surrounding marine environments promote nutrient cycling, supporting productivity in adjacent ecosystems such as seagrass meadows and mangroves.

Economically, coral reefs are invaluable to millions of people who depend on them for their livelihoods. They underpin industries such as tourism, fishing, and recreation, generating billions of dollars annually. Tourists are drawn to the beauty and biodiversity of coral reefs, supporting local economies through activities such as snorkeling, scuba diving, and eco-tourism ventures. In many coastal regions, reef-related tourism provides a significant source of income and employment, creating a direct link between reef health and economic stability.

The cultural and social importance of coral reefs is another aspect of their value. For many coastal and island communities, coral reefs hold deep cultural significance, serving as symbols of identity and heritage. Traditional fishing practices, rituals, and folklore are often tied to reef ecosystems, highlighting their integral role in the cultural fabric of these societies.

Despite their importance, coral reefs are among the most threatened ecosystems in the world. Climate change, pollution, overfishing, and unsustainable development have contributed to widespread reef degradation. Ocean warming and acidification, caused by increasing levels of atmospheric carbon dioxide, have led to coral bleaching and reduced reef resilience. Local stressors such as sedimentation, nutrient runoff, and destructive fishing practices further compound these threats, jeopardizing the ability of reefs to provide their critical ecosystem services.

The decline of coral reefs has far-reaching consequences for marine ecosystems and human communities alike. Loss of biodiversity, reduced fish stocks, and diminished coastal protection are just some of the cascading impacts of reef degradation. Protecting and restoring coral reefs is therefore not only an ecological imperative but also a societal and economic necessity.

Nature-Based Solutions for Coral Reef Restoration (Gardening, Artificial Reefs, Micro-Fragmentation)

Coral reefs are vital ecosystems that support marine biodiversity, provide coastal protection, and sustain millions of people through fisheries and tourism. However, these ecosystems face unprecedented threats from climate change, pollution, overfishing, and habitat destruction. To address this degradation, NbS have emerged as effective approaches for restoring coral reefs. This section focuses on three widely implemented NbS techniques for coral reef restoration: coral gardening, artificial reefs, and micro-fragmentation. Each technique plays a crucial role in enhancing reef resilience, biodiversity, and functionality.

Coral Gardening

Coral gardening is one of the most effective and widely used techniques for coral reef restoration. It involves growing coral fragments in a controlled environment, such as an underwater nursery, and later transplanting them onto degraded reef areas. This method mimics natural coral reproduction and growth, accelerating the recovery of damaged reefs.

The process begins with the collection of coral fragments, often broken pieces that would otherwise die if left on the seafloor. These fragments are carefully selected from healthy donor colonies to ensure genetic diversity and resilience. Once collected, the fragments are transported to underwater or land-based nurseries, where they are attached to structures such as ropes, frames, or racks. These nurseries provide an optimal environment for corals to grow, protecting them from predation and unfavorable conditions.

Once the coral fragments reach a suitable size, they are transplanted onto degraded reef areas. The transplantation process involves securely attaching the fragments to the substrate using marine epoxy, zip ties, or natural binding methods. Over time, the corals grow and integrate into the existing reef, enhancing its structure and ecological function.

Coral gardening is highly adaptable and can be used for a variety of coral species. It is particularly effective in areas where natural recovery is slow or hindered by environmental stressors. However, the technique requires ongoing maintenance, such as cleaning the nursery structures and monitoring the transplanted corals. Despite these challenges, coral gardening has been successful in restoring degraded reefs worldwide, making it a cornerstone of coral restoration efforts.

Artificial Reefs

Artificial reefs are human-made structures designed to mimic the characteristics of natural coral reefs, providing a substrate for coral growth and habitat for marine life. These structures can be made from a variety of materials, including concrete, steel, limestone, and even repurposed objects such as ships or airplanes. By creating a foundation for coral colonization, artificial reefs help restore ecological function in degraded areas.

The design and placement of artificial reefs are critical to their success. Structures must be carefully engineered to withstand ocean currents, provide suitable surfaces for coral attachment, and encourage biodiversity. Many artificial reefs are designed with features such as holes, crevices, and ledges to replicate the complexity of natural reefs. The location of the reef is also important, as it must align with the environmental conditions required for coral growth, such as light availability, water temperature, and nutrient levels.

Artificial reefs offer several advantages for coral restoration. They provide immediate habitat for fish and invertebrates, helping to rebuild reef communities while corals grow and colonize the structures. Additionally, they can be strategically placed to protect shorelines from wave energy, reducing coastal erosion.

While artificial reefs are effective in many scenarios, they are not without limitations. Poorly designed or improperly placed structures can disrupt natural ecosystems or fail to support coral growth. To address these issues, researchers and practitioners are increasingly using eco-friendly materials and innovative designs, such as 3D-printed reefs, to enhance the functionality and sustainability of artificial reefs.

Micro-Fragmentation

Micro-fragmentation is a groundbreaking technique that accelerates coral growth by taking advantage of their natural healing processes. This method involves breaking coral colonies into small fragments, typically less than a few centimeters in size, and allowing them to regenerate. Unlike traditional restoration methods, micro-fragmentation significantly speeds up the growth rate of certain coral species, particularly slow-growing ones such as massive corals.

The process begins with the selection of donor corals, which are carefully fragmented into tiny pieces using precision tools. These fragments are then attached to specially designed substrates, such as ceramic tiles or concrete discs, in a controlled environment. The fragments grow rapidly as they fuse together, forming larger colonies within months instead of years. Once sufficiently grown, these colonies are transplanted onto degraded reef areas, where they continue to expand and integrate into the existing reef structure.

Micro-fragmentation is especially valuable for restoring corals that have been heavily impacted by bleaching events or disease outbreaks. It also allows for the propagation of resilient coral genotypes, enhancing the adaptive capacity of restored reefs. However, the technique requires skilled labor and infrastructure, such as aquaculture facilities, making it more resource-intensive than other methods.

Despite its challenges, micro-fragmentation has demonstrated remarkable success in restoring coral cover and enhancing reef resilience. It is often used in combination with other NbS techniques, such as coral gardening, to maximize restoration outcomes.

Integration and Future Potential of NbS Techniques

The effectiveness of coral reef restoration often depends on the integration of multiple NbS techniques. For example, coral gardening can be combined with micro-fragmentation to propagate both fast-growing and slow-growing species, ensuring ecological diversity. Similarly, artificial reefs can provide a stable substrate for transplanted corals, enhancing their survival and growth.

The success of these techniques also relies on addressing broader challenges, such as water quality management, climate change mitigation, and community engagement. Ensuring that restoration efforts align with long-term conservation goals and involve local stakeholders is critical for their sustainability.

Emerging technologies and innovations continue to enhance the potential of NbS for coral reef restoration. Advancements in 3D printing, genetic research, and robotics offer new opportunities to scale up restoration efforts and improve their efficiency. By combining traditional methods with cutting-edge technologies, practitioners can better address the complex challenges facing coral reefs.

Addressing Threats Like Warming and Acidification

Climate change poses some of the most significant and immediate threats to coral reefs, particularly through ocean warming and acidification. These processes are primarily driven by the increasing concentration of greenhouse gases in the atmosphere, resulting in rising sea temperatures and changes in ocean chemistry. Together, these threats have led to widespread coral bleaching, loss of biodiversity, and diminished reef resilience. Addressing these challenges requires a combination of local conservation efforts, global mitigation strategies, and innovative restoration approaches.

The Impact of Ocean Warming on Coral Reefs

Ocean warming is one of the most direct consequences of climate change and has a profound impact on coral reefs. Corals rely on a symbiotic relationship with microscopic algae called zooxanthellae, which live within their tissues. These algae provide corals with much of their energy through photosynthesis, while corals offer the algae protection and access to sunlight. However, when sea temperatures rise beyond the tolerance levels of corals, this delicate relationship breaks down. The stress causes corals to expel their algae, resulting in a phenomenon known as coral bleaching. Without the algae, corals lose their primary energy source, turning white and becoming highly vulnerable to disease and mortality.

Bleaching events have become increasingly frequent and severe in recent decades. For example, mass bleaching events associated with elevated sea temperatures during El Niño years have devastated coral reefs around the globe. The Great Barrier Reef, one of the largest reef systems in the world, has experienced significant coral loss due to repeated bleaching events. If warming trends continue, it is estimated that many coral species may face extinction within the century.

The Role of Ocean Acidification

Ocean acidification is another major threat to coral reefs. As the ocean absorbs carbon dioxide (CO_2) from the atmosphere, chemical reactions occur that reduce the pH of seawater, making it more acidic. This process also decreases the availability of carbonate ions, which are essential for corals to build and maintain their calcium carbonate skeletons. Without sufficient carbonate ions, corals struggle to grow, and their skeletons become more susceptible to erosion.

Acidification not only weakens coral structures but also affects the broader reef ecosystem. Species that rely on reefs for habitat and food, such as fish and invertebrates, are also impacted. Furthermore, acidification alters predator-prey dynamics and the behavior of marine organisms, disrupting the ecological balance of reef systems. Combined with warming, acidification exacerbates the stress on coral reefs, making it one of the most critical challenges to address.

Strategies to Mitigate Ocean Warming and Acidification

Efforts to address the threats of ocean warming and acidification must occur at both global and local levels. At the global scale, reducing greenhouse gas emissions is essential to limit the extent of warming and acidification. International agreements like the Paris Agreement aim to achieve this by setting targets for reducing CO_2 emissions and limiting global temperature increases. Meeting these targets requires collective action from governments, industries, and individuals to transition to renewable energy sources, improve energy efficiency, and adopt sustainable practices.

Locally, coral reef conservation efforts can help mitigate the impacts of warming and acidification by improving the resilience of reef ecosystems. For example, managing water quality is critical for reducing stress on corals. Nutrient runoff from agriculture and untreated wastewater can exacerbate the effects of warming by promoting algal blooms and reducing oxygen levels. Implementing better land-use practices and improving wastewater treatment can significantly enhance reef health.

Another effective strategy is the establishment of marine protected areas (MPAs) that limit activities such as fishing, tourism, and coastal development in sensitive reef zones. MPAs provide corals with a refuge from additional stressors, allowing them to recover and maintain their ecological functions. When designed and enforced effectively, MPAs have been shown to increase coral cover, biodiversity, and fish populations, contributing to the overall resilience of reef ecosystems.

Innovative Approaches to Enhance Coral Resilience

In addition to mitigation and conservation efforts, innovative approaches are being developed to enhance coral resilience to warming and acidification. One such approach is the selective breeding of heat-resistant corals. By identifying and propagating coral species or genotypes that can tolerate higher temperatures, scientists aim to create "super corals" capable of surviving in warmer waters. These resilient corals can then be used in restoration projects to establish more robust reef systems.

Another promising technique is assisted evolution, which involves accelerating the natural adaptation processes of corals. This can include exposing corals to controlled stressors to increase their tolerance to environmental changes or manipulating their symbiotic algae to improve thermal resistance. While these methods are still in the experimental stage, they offer hope for developing more resilient reef ecosystems in the face of climate change.

Geoengineering solutions, such as shading reefs with reflective materials or pumping cooler water onto overheated reefs, have also been proposed as emergency measures to prevent bleaching during extreme heat events. While these interventions are not long-term solutions, they could provide temporary relief for coral reefs during critical periods.

The Path Forward

Addressing the threats of warming and acidification to coral reefs requires a comprehensive approach that combines global emissions reductions, local conservation efforts, and innovative restoration techniques. While significant challenges remain, the development of new technologies and the growing recognition of the importance of coral reefs provide a strong foundation for action.

Chapter 3: Seagrass Meadows for Marine Biodiversity

Seagrass meadows, often overshadowed by more iconic coastal ecosystems like coral reefs and mangroves, are among the most productive and ecologically significant habitats in the marine environment. Found in shallow coastal waters, these submerged flowering plants form extensive underwater meadows that provide critical services to both marine life and human communities. Seagrass meadows are biodiversity hotspots, supporting a wide array of species, including fish, crustaceans, and marine mammals. They also play a vital role in carbon sequestration, nutrient cycling, and sediment stabilization.

This chapter explores the importance of seagrass meadows as pillars of marine biodiversity and ecosystem health. It delves into the ecological functions of seagrass ecosystems, highlighting their role as nursery habitats and their contributions to the productivity of adjacent ecosystems like coral reefs and mangroves. Additionally, the chapter examines the threats facing seagrass meadows, from coastal development to climate change, and discusses NbS for their conservation and restoration.

By understanding the ecological value of seagrass meadows and the strategies for protecting and restoring them, this chapter emphasizes their essential role in maintaining healthy marine ecosystems and fostering coastal resilience.

Functions of Seagrass Meadows in Coastal Ecosystems

Seagrass meadows are among the most vital ecosystems in the marine environment, providing a range of ecological, economic, and social benefits. These underwater meadows, composed of flowering plants adapted to marine conditions, are found in shallow coastal waters worldwide, often in proximity to coral reefs, mangroves, and salt marshes. Despite covering only a small fraction of the ocean floor, seagrass meadows play a disproportionately large role in maintaining the health and productivity of coastal ecosystems.

Habitat Provision and Biodiversity Support

One of the most significant functions of seagrass meadows is their role as critical habitats for a diverse array of marine species. The dense, interwoven structure of seagrass blades provides shelter and protection from predators, particularly for juvenile fish, crustaceans, and invertebrates. Many commercially important fish species, such as snapper, grouper, and shrimp, use seagrass meadows as nursery grounds during early stages of their life cycles. By offering food and refuge, seagrass meadows contribute to the sustainability of fisheries that support millions of livelihoods.

Seagrass meadows also host a variety of species that are unique to these ecosystems, such as sea urchins, pipefish, and certain species of seahorses. Larger marine animals, including dugongs, manatees, and green sea turtles, depend on seagrass as a primary food source. The high biodiversity found in seagrass meadows makes them essential for maintaining ecological balance and the resilience of coastal ecosystems.

Carbon Sequestration and Climate Regulation

Seagrass meadows play a significant role in mitigating climate change through their ability to sequester carbon dioxide from the atmosphere. Often referred to as "blue carbon" ecosystems, seagrasses store carbon in their biomass and, more importantly, in the sediments beneath them. The dense root systems of seagrasses trap organic matter and sediments, creating long-term carbon storage that can persist for centuries.

On a per-area basis, seagrass meadows can sequester carbon at rates comparable to or even greater than terrestrial forests. This capacity to act as a carbon sink makes them an invaluable asset in global efforts to reduce greenhouse gas concentrations. However, when seagrass meadows are degraded or destroyed, the stored carbon is released back into the atmosphere, contributing to climate change. Protecting and restoring seagrass ecosystems is therefore critical for maintaining their climate regulation functions.

Water Quality Improvement

Seagrass meadows play an essential role in maintaining water quality in coastal areas. The leaves and root systems of seagrass plants act as natural filters, trapping suspended particles, nutrients, and pollutants in the water column. This process reduces turbidity and improves light penetration, benefiting other marine ecosystems such as coral reefs that rely on clear water for photosynthesis.

Additionally, seagrasses help regulate nutrient levels in coastal waters. Excess nutrients from agricultural runoff and wastewater can lead to algal blooms and hypoxic conditions, which are harmful to marine life. Seagrasses absorb these nutrients, preventing eutrophication and maintaining a balanced nutrient cycle. By improving water clarity and quality, seagrass meadows support the overall health of coastal ecosystems.

Sediment Stabilization and Coastal Protection

Seagrass meadows play a crucial role in stabilizing coastal sediments and protecting shorelines from erosion. The dense root systems of seagrasses bind sediments to the seafloor, reducing their resuspension by waves and currents. This stabilization prevents sediment from being carried away, maintaining the integrity of coastal landscapes.

Furthermore, the leaves of seagrass plants reduce wave energy as it passes over the meadow, minimizing the impact of waves on the shoreline. This function is particularly important in protecting coastal areas from the effects of storms, sea-level rise, and human activities that exacerbate erosion. By acting as a natural barrier, seagrass meadows enhance coastal resilience and reduce the need for costly man-made infrastructure.

Connectivity with Adjacent Ecosystems

Seagrass meadows are highly interconnected with other coastal ecosystems, such as coral reefs and mangroves, forming a network of habitats that support marine life. These ecosystems rely on one another for the exchange of nutrients, energy, and species. For example, many fish and invertebrates migrate between seagrass meadows, coral reefs, and mangroves during different stages of their life cycles.

This connectivity enhances the productivity and resilience of the entire coastal ecosystem. The health of seagrass meadows directly impacts the functioning of adjacent habitats, emphasizing the need to manage these ecosystems as integrated systems rather than in isolation.

Economic and Cultural Importance

In addition to their ecological functions, seagrass meadows provide significant economic and cultural benefits. By supporting fisheries, tourism, and recreational activities, these ecosystems contribute to the livelihoods of millions of people. Seagrass meadows are also culturally significant for many coastal communities, serving as sources of traditional knowledge, practices, and spiritual connections to nature.

Restoration Techniques for Seagrass Meadows (Transplantation, Seed Dispersal, Water Quality Improvements)

Seagrass meadows are vital coastal ecosystems that provide critical ecological, economic, and social benefits. However, they are increasingly under threat from human activities such as coastal development, pollution, and climate change, leading to significant degradation and loss. To address this, various restoration techniques have been developed to rehabilitate seagrass meadows and ensure their ecological functions are preserved. This section explores three key restoration techniques: transplantation, seed dispersal, and water quality improvements, highlighting their processes, benefits, and challenges.

Transplantation

Transplantation is one of the most widely used methods for restoring seagrass meadows. This technique involves the direct transfer of healthy seagrass plants or shoots from donor sites to degraded or barren areas. The goal is to establish a vegetative cover that can grow and expand, ultimately restoring the ecosystem's functions and benefits.

The transplantation process typically begins with the identification of a suitable donor site. This site must have a robust and healthy seagrass population, as removing plants should not jeopardize its ecological integrity. Once the donor site is selected, individual seagrass shoots or clumps are harvested, usually by hand or with specialized tools to minimize disturbance to the surrounding environment.

The harvested seagrass is then transported to the restoration site, where it is carefully planted in the substrate. Various planting techniques can be employed, depending on site conditions. For example, seagrass shoots can be anchored using biodegradable stakes, weighted grids, or mesh frames to prevent them from being dislodged by currents or waves. In some cases, seagrass clumps are bundled and inserted into prepared holes in the sediment to ensure stability.

While transplantation is effective in many scenarios, it is labor-intensive and requires careful planning. The success of this technique depends on factors such as substrate suitability, water depth, and light availability. Additionally, the harvesting of seagrass from donor sites must be carefully managed to avoid over-exploitation and ensure the sustainability of the donor population.

Seed Dispersal

Seed dispersal is another important technique for restoring seagrass meadows, particularly in areas where natural seagrass populations have been lost entirely. This method focuses on promoting the natural reproductive processes of seagrass plants by collecting and distributing seeds to restoration sites. Seed dispersal can be a cost-effective alternative to transplantation and has the potential to restore large areas of seagrass habitat.

The process begins with the collection of seeds from existing seagrass meadows. This is often done during the flowering and fruiting season when seagrass plants produce viable seeds. Seeds can be collected manually by divers or through the use of nets and traps placed in the water column to capture floating seeds.

Once collected, the seeds are prepared for dispersal. Depending on the restoration strategy, seeds can be sown directly onto the sediment at the restoration site or grown in nurseries until they germinate and develop into seedlings. Direct sowing is typically carried out in areas with stable substrates and low wave energy, where seeds are less likely to be displaced. In contrast, growing seedlings in nurseries allows for better control over environmental conditions, increasing the chances of successful establishment.

Seed dispersal offers several advantages over transplantation. It is less labor-intensive and can cover larger areas, making it particularly useful for large-scale restoration projects. Additionally, seeds can be sourced from multiple donor sites, increasing genetic diversity and resilience in the restored population. However, seed dispersal also presents challenges, such as ensuring adequate seed viability, overcoming predation by marine organisms, and managing environmental conditions that influence germination and growth.

Water Quality Improvements

Improving water quality is a foundational step in restoring seagrass meadows, as degraded water conditions are often the primary cause of seagrass loss. Seagrasses require clear water with sufficient light penetration for photosynthesis, as well as balanced nutrient levels to support healthy growth. Addressing water quality issues not only facilitates successful restoration but also ensures the long-term sustainability of restored meadows.

The first step in improving water quality is identifying the sources of pollution affecting the restoration site. Common sources include agricultural runoff, wastewater discharge, and sedimentation from coastal development. Once the sources are identified, targeted interventions can be implemented to reduce or eliminate these pollutants.

Nutrient management is a critical aspect of water quality improvement. Excess nutrients, particularly nitrogen and phosphorus, can lead to algal blooms that block sunlight and deplete oxygen levels, making it difficult for seagrass to thrive. Strategies to reduce nutrient inputs include promoting sustainable agricultural practices, upgrading wastewater treatment facilities, and implementing buffer zones along waterways to filter runoff before it reaches coastal areas.

Sediment control is another key factor in improving water quality. Excess sedimentation can smother seagrass beds and reduce light availability. Measures such as reforestation of coastal watersheds, installation of silt fences, and regulation of dredging activities can help minimize sediment inputs to restoration sites.

In some cases, direct interventions may be needed to address existing water quality issues at the restoration site. For example, aeration or oxygenation systems can be used to improve dissolved oxygen levels in areas affected by hypoxia. Additionally, the removal of accumulated sediments or algae may be necessary to create suitable conditions for seagrass growth.

Water quality improvements are often undertaken in conjunction with other restoration techniques, such as transplantation or seed dispersal, to maximize their effectiveness. By addressing the root causes of seagrass loss, these interventions create a supportive environment for restored meadows to establish and flourish.

Integrating Restoration Techniques

In practice, successful seagrass restoration often involves a combination of these techniques. For example, water quality improvements may be implemented first to create suitable conditions, followed by transplantation or seed dispersal to establish seagrass cover. The choice of techniques depends on site-specific conditions, such as the extent of degradation, availability of donor material, and environmental factors.

Monitoring and adaptive management are essential components of any restoration effort. Regular monitoring allows practitioners to assess the success of restoration techniques and make necessary adjustments to address challenges or changing conditions. By integrating scientific knowledge, community involvement, and innovative practices, seagrass restoration can achieve long-lasting ecological and social benefits.

Integrating Seagrass Conservation with Coastal Planning

Seagrass meadows are vital coastal ecosystems that provide significant ecological, economic, and social benefits. However, they face numerous threats from urbanization, coastal development, pollution, and climate change. Integrating seagrass conservation into broader coastal planning efforts is essential to ensure their protection and the sustainability of the services they provide. By aligning conservation goals with coastal development strategies, it is possible to balance ecological preservation with human needs.

The Importance of Coastal Planning for Seagrass Conservation

Coastal planning is the process of managing human activities along coastlines to minimize environmental impacts and ensure sustainable use of resources. Given the location of seagrass meadows in shallow coastal waters, they are often affected by development activities, such as construction of ports, resorts, and infrastructure. Without proper planning, these activities can result in habitat destruction, increased sedimentation, and pollution, all of which threaten seagrass ecosystems.

Integrating seagrass conservation into coastal planning ensures that these ecosystems are considered in development decisions. This approach recognizes the interconnected nature of coastal environments and aims to protect the ecological functions of seagrass meadows while allowing for responsible human activities. By doing so, it is possible to mitigate conflicts between conservation and development and promote long-term sustainability.

Key Strategies for Integrating Seagrass Conservation

1. Incorporating Seagrass Mapping into Coastal Planning

The first step in integrating seagrass conservation with coastal planning is to identify and map the locations of seagrass meadows. Accurate and up-to-date maps provide valuable information about the extent, health, and distribution of these ecosystems. This data can inform decision-making processes, such as zoning and land-use planning, ensuring that development activities avoid critical seagrass habitats. Advanced technologies, such as satellite imagery, remote sensing, and underwater drones, have improved the ability to monitor and map seagrass meadows efficiently.

2. Establishing MPAs

Marine Protected Areas are an effective tool for safeguarding seagrass meadows from harmful activities. MPAs can be designed to include seagrass habitats, restricting activities such as dredging, bottom trawling, and unregulated tourism that can damage these ecosystems. Properly enforced MPAs not only protect seagrass meadows but also enhance the resilience of coastal ecosystems as a whole. Integrating MPAs into coastal planning ensures that these conservation zones are strategically placed to maximize their ecological and social benefits.

3. Implementing Environmental Impact Assessments (EIAs)

Environmental Impact Assessments are essential for evaluating the potential effects of development projects on seagrass meadows. EIAs should be mandatory for any coastal development activity, ensuring that the impacts on seagrass ecosystems are thoroughly assessed before projects are approved. Developers can use this information to design projects that minimize habitat disruption, such as adjusting construction timelines, using sediment control measures, or relocating activities away from sensitive areas.

4. Promoting Sustainable Coastal Development Practices

Sustainable coastal development practices aim to reduce the environmental footprint of human activities. For seagrass conservation, this may include minimizing dredging and land reclamation, using eco-friendly construction materials, and employing technologies that reduce pollution. For example, using silt curtains during construction can prevent sedimentation from smothering seagrass meadows. Sustainable practices ensure that development activities can coexist with the preservation of seagrass ecosystems.

5. Integrating Seagrass into Climate Adaptation Plans

Seagrass meadows play a critical role in climate resilience by stabilizing sediments, reducing coastal erosion, and sequestering carbon. Coastal planning should incorporate seagrass conservation into climate adaptation strategies to enhance the resilience of coastal communities. For example, restoring and protecting seagrass meadows can provide natural buffers against storm surges and sea-level rise, reducing the reliance on costly man-made infrastructure.

Challenges in Integrating Seagrass Conservation

Despite the benefits of integrating seagrass conservation with coastal planning, several challenges exist. One significant barrier is the lack of awareness about the importance of seagrass ecosystems among policymakers, developers, and the public. This often leads to their undervaluation in decision-making processes. Increasing public education and advocacy can help highlight the ecological and economic benefits of seagrass conservation.

Another challenge is the lack of coordination among stakeholders involved in coastal planning. Seagrass conservation requires collaboration between multiple sectors, including fisheries, tourism, agriculture, and urban development. Fragmented governance structures and conflicting interests can hinder effective integration. Establishing clear policies, communication channels, and multi-stakeholder platforms can address these challenges and foster cooperation.

Insufficient funding for seagrass conservation and monitoring is another limitation. Coastal planning processes often prioritize economic development over environmental protection, resulting in inadequate resources for conservation initiatives. Innovative financing mechanisms, such as PES and public-private partnerships, can provide the necessary funding to support seagrass conservation efforts.

The Path Forward

Integrating seagrass conservation with coastal planning requires a holistic and proactive approach. Policymakers, planners, and stakeholders must recognize the value of seagrass meadows and their role in supporting biodiversity, mitigating climate change, and sustaining livelihoods. By adopting strategies such as seagrass mapping, MPAs, EIAs, sustainable development practices, and climate adaptation plans, it is possible to protect these ecosystems while meeting human needs.

Education, stakeholder collaboration, and innovative financing are critical to overcoming challenges and ensuring the success of integrated planning efforts. As coastal areas continue to face pressures from development and climate change, prioritizing seagrass conservation in planning processes will be essential for maintaining the health and resilience of coastal ecosystems.

Chapter 4: Salt Marshes for Flood Mitigation

Salt marshes, characterized by their dense vegetation and proximity to tidal waters, are among the most effective natural systems for mitigating floods and protecting coastal communities. These ecosystems, often found in temperate and subtropical regions, play a critical role in buffering coastlines from storm surges, reducing wave energy, and stabilizing sediments. Their ability to absorb and store water makes them invaluable in managing both coastal and inland flooding.

This chapter explores the functions of salt marshes in flood mitigation, emphasizing their ecological and protective roles. It examines the processes that enable salt marshes to act as natural flood defenses and discusses how they complement man-made infrastructure in reducing the impacts of extreme weather events. Additionally, the chapter highlights restoration and conservation techniques that enhance the flood-mitigation capacity of salt marshes while addressing threats such as climate change, urbanization, and pollution.

By understanding the unique role of salt marshes in flood management, this chapter underscores their importance as a Nature-Based Solution for building resilient coastlines and adapting to a changing climate.

Ecological Roles of Salt Marshes

Salt marshes are dynamic ecosystems located in coastal intertidal zones, where they provide essential ecological functions that benefit both the environment and human communities. Dominated by salt-tolerant vegetation, such as grasses and shrubs, salt marshes thrive in areas subject to regular tidal flooding. Despite their often-overlooked status, salt marshes play a vital role in maintaining coastal and marine ecosystem health, contributing significantly to biodiversity, nutrient cycling, carbon sequestration, and sediment stabilization.

Biodiversity Support

Salt marshes are biodiversity hotspots, supporting a wide range of plant and animal species. The vegetation in salt marshes provides habitat and shelter for various organisms, including invertebrates, fish, birds, and mammals. Many commercially and ecologically important fish and shellfish species, such as blue crabs, shrimp, and mullet, use salt marshes as nursery grounds, where they find abundant food and protection from predators.

Migratory birds rely heavily on salt marshes as resting and feeding sites during their long journeys. Species such as herons, egrets, and sandpipers are commonly found in these habitats, where they forage for invertebrates and small fish. The presence of diverse plant species in salt marshes also supports populations of insects, which in turn serve as food for higher trophic levels. This interconnected web of life highlights the importance of salt marshes in sustaining coastal biodiversity.

Nutrient Cycling and Water Quality

Salt marshes play a crucial role in nutrient cycling, helping to regulate the flow of nitrogen, phosphorus, and other nutrients between terrestrial and aquatic environments. The plants and microbial communities in salt marshes absorb excess nutrients from the water, preventing nutrient overload in coastal waters. This process reduces the risk of eutrophication, a condition in which excessive nutrients lead to algal blooms, oxygen depletion, and the creation of "dead zones" where aquatic life cannot survive.

In addition to nutrient cycling, salt marshes improve water quality by filtering sediments, pollutants, and heavy metals. Tidal flows allow water to move through the marsh vegetation, where sediments and contaminants settle out and are trapped by plant roots. This natural filtration system protects downstream ecosystems, such as estuaries and coral reefs, from the harmful effects of sedimentation and pollution.

Carbon Sequestration and Climate Regulation

Salt marshes are highly effective at sequestering carbon, making them an important natural ally in mitigating climate change. Known as "blue carbon" ecosystems, salt marshes capture and store carbon dioxide from the atmosphere in their plants and sediments. The dense root systems of marsh vegetation stabilize organic matter in the soil, where it can remain sequestered for centuries or even millennia.

On a per-area basis, salt marshes can sequester carbon at rates comparable to or greater than terrestrial forests. This ability to store carbon not only helps offset greenhouse gas emissions but also enhances the resilience of salt marshes themselves, enabling them to keep pace with sea-level rise through sediment accumulation. However, when salt marshes are degraded or lost, the stored carbon is released back into the atmosphere, contributing to climate change.

Sediment Stabilization and Coastal Protection

Salt marshes are essential for stabilizing coastal sediments and protecting shorelines from erosion. The dense root systems of salt marsh plants bind sediments to the substrate, reducing their susceptibility to erosion by tidal flows, currents, and storms. This stabilization helps maintain the integrity of coastal landscapes, preventing land loss and protecting infrastructure.

Additionally, the above-ground vegetation in salt marshes reduces wave energy as water flows over the marsh. This wave attenuation function diminishes the impact of storm surges and high tides on adjacent coastal areas, acting as a natural barrier against flooding. By buffering coastlines from the effects of extreme weather events, salt marshes enhance the resilience of coastal communities to climate change and sea-level rise.

Connectivity with Adjacent Ecosystems

Salt marshes are intrinsically connected to other coastal ecosystems, such as estuaries, seagrass meadows, and mangroves, forming a network of habitats that support marine and terrestrial life. Nutrient exchange between salt marshes and adjacent ecosystems enhances productivity, while the movement of species between habitats ensures ecological balance.

For example, salt marshes often serve as feeding grounds for fish and invertebrates that inhabit nearby seagrass meadows or coral reefs. The health of these interconnected ecosystems depends on the proper functioning of salt marshes, emphasizing their importance in maintaining coastal biodiversity and ecological resilience.

Restoration Strategies for Salt Marshes (Sediment Augmentation, Vegetation Planting)

Salt marshes are vital coastal ecosystems that provide essential ecological services, including flood mitigation, carbon sequestration, biodiversity support, and water quality improvement. However, these ecosystems are increasingly threatened by human activities, such as coastal development, pollution, and habitat alteration, as well as by climate change impacts like sea-level rise and extreme weather events. Restoration strategies, such as sediment augmentation and vegetation planting, play a critical role in rehabilitating degraded salt marshes and ensuring their long-term sustainability.

Sediment Augmentation

Sediment augmentation is a restoration technique that addresses one of the primary challenges facing salt marshes: the loss of elevation due to sediment depletion, sea-level rise, or human activities. This approach involves the deliberate addition of sediment to degraded salt marshes to raise their elevation and create suitable conditions for marsh vegetation to grow.

The process begins with a careful assessment of the site to determine the amount and type of sediment required. Factors such as the local tidal range, salinity, and sediment grain size are critical in selecting appropriate materials for augmentation. Sediment can be sourced from dredged materials, nearby waterways, or offshore sites, provided it meets environmental safety standards and is free of contaminants.

Once the sediment is sourced, it is transported to the restoration site and applied to the marsh surface. Methods of application vary depending on site conditions and project goals. Thin-layer deposition is a common technique, where sediment is evenly spread across the marsh surface to mimic natural sedimentation processes. This approach minimizes disruption to existing vegetation and allows for gradual elevation gain.

Sediment augmentation provides several ecological benefits. By restoring elevation, it helps salt marshes maintain their position within the intertidal zone, where they can continue to support diverse plant and animal communities. Additionally, sediment addition promotes the accumulation of organic matter, which enhances soil stability and nutrient availability for vegetation. Restoring elevation also improves the marsh's ability to absorb wave energy and reduce flooding in adjacent areas.

Despite its benefits, sediment augmentation poses challenges. The sourcing and transport of sediment can be costly and logistically complex, particularly for large-scale projects. Moreover, the potential impacts of sediment deposition on nearby ecosystems, such as seagrass beds or coral reefs, must be carefully managed. Monitoring and adaptive management are essential to ensure that sediment augmentation achieves its intended outcomes without causing unintended ecological harm.

Vegetation Planting

Vegetation planting is another key restoration strategy for salt marshes, focusing on re-establishing salt-tolerant plants that are essential for stabilizing sediments, supporting biodiversity, and providing ecosystem services. This technique is particularly effective in areas where natural regeneration is limited due to severe degradation or ongoing disturbances.

The restoration process begins with the selection of appropriate plant species for the site. Salt marsh vegetation typically consists of halophytic (salt-tolerant) plants such as cordgrass (*Spartina* species), pickleweed (*Salicornia*), and saltgrass (*Distichlis*). Selecting native species that are well-adapted to local environmental conditions is crucial for ensuring high survival rates and ecological compatibility.

Once species are selected, planting materials are prepared. These may include seeds, seedlings, or mature plants, depending on the project's goals and timeline. In some cases, plant material is propagated in nurseries to ensure a consistent supply and healthy stock for restoration efforts.

Planting techniques vary based on site conditions and project objectives. In areas with stable sediments, seeds can be directly sown into the soil, while in more dynamic environments, seedlings or mature plants may be transplanted for greater stability. Spacing and planting density are carefully planned to allow for natural expansion and to optimize the marsh's ecological functions.

Vegetation planting provides immediate and long-term benefits to salt marsh ecosystems. The roots of salt marsh plants stabilize sediments, reducing erosion and enhancing the marsh's ability to withstand tidal flows and storm surges. Above-ground vegetation traps sediments and nutrients, supporting soil formation and nutrient cycling. Over time, the re-established vegetation creates a habitat for a wide range of organisms, from invertebrates to birds, contributing to the overall biodiversity of the ecosystem.

However, vegetation planting is not without challenges. Success depends on site conditions such as salinity, hydrology, and sediment composition. Extreme weather events, such as storms or prolonged droughts, can damage newly planted vegetation and impede restoration progress. Moreover, competition from invasive species may threaten the establishment of native plants. Ongoing monitoring and maintenance, including invasive species control and replanting efforts, are critical for overcoming these challenges and ensuring the success of vegetation restoration.

Integration of Sediment Augmentation and Vegetation Planting

In many restoration projects, sediment augmentation and vegetation planting are combined to maximize ecological outcomes. Sediment augmentation provides a stable substrate with the appropriate elevation for planting, while vegetation establishment enhances sediment stability and promotes the recovery of ecosystem functions. This integrated approach is particularly effective in heavily degraded salt marshes where both elevation loss and vegetation decline have occurred.

For example, after applying sediment through augmentation, vegetation planting can be carried out to expedite the recovery process. Plant roots help bind the newly added sediment, reducing erosion and allowing the marsh to adapt to future environmental changes. Additionally, the presence of vegetation accelerates the accumulation of organic matter, further enhancing soil quality and ecosystem resilience.

Challenges and Future Directions

Both sediment augmentation and vegetation planting face challenges that require careful planning and adaptive management. Funding constraints, logistical complexities, and environmental uncertainties can hinder restoration efforts. Furthermore, long-term success depends on addressing the root causes of salt marsh degradation, such as pollution, altered hydrology, and climate change.

Innovations in restoration science and technology offer new opportunities to overcome these challenges. For instance, the use of drones for mapping and monitoring, genetic techniques to enhance plant resilience, and collaborations with local communities to integrate traditional knowledge can significantly improve restoration outcomes. Incorporating these advancements into restoration strategies ensures that salt marsh restoration efforts remain effective and sustainable.

Addressing Challenges in Salt Marsh Restoration (Sea-Level Rise, Invasive Species)

Salt marshes are essential coastal ecosystems, offering critical services such as flood protection, carbon sequestration, and biodiversity support. However, they face significant challenges from environmental and anthropogenic pressures. Two major issues threatening the survival and restoration of salt marshes are sea-level rise and invasive species. Addressing these challenges requires targeted strategies that combine ecological understanding, innovative approaches, and effective management practices.

Challenge 1: Sea-Level Rise

Sea-level rise is one of the most pressing threats to salt marshes, driven by climate change and the thermal expansion of oceans. As sea levels rise, salt marshes can become submerged, reducing their ability to function as intertidal ecosystems. This can lead to a loss of vegetation, decreased biodiversity, and a decline in their flood-mitigation capabilities. If salt marshes cannot maintain elevation through natural sediment deposition or migrate landward, they risk being permanently inundated.

One strategy to address sea-level rise is sediment augmentation, a technique that adds sediment to salt marshes to help them maintain elevation. By raising the marsh surface, sediment augmentation allows marsh vegetation to remain in the intertidal zone, where it can continue to thrive. This process can be further enhanced by planting salt-tolerant vegetation that promotes sediment trapping and organic matter accumulation, boosting the marsh's ability to adapt to rising seas.

Facilitating landward migration is another important approach. As sea levels rise, salt marshes naturally migrate inland to maintain their position relative to tidal inundation. However, human development, such as roads, seawalls, and urban infrastructure, often blocks this migration. Coastal planning and land-use policies should prioritize the creation of buffer zones or managed retreat programs that allow salt marshes to shift landward. These measures ensure that marsh ecosystems can adapt to changing conditions without being lost to rising waters.

Monitoring and predictive modeling are also essential for managing the impacts of sea-level rise. Regular assessments of marsh elevation, sediment deposition rates, and tidal inundation patterns can help identify areas at risk of submersion. Using predictive models, restoration practitioners can forecast future changes and implement proactive measures to safeguard vulnerable salt marshes.

Challenge 2: Invasive Species

Invasive species are another major threat to salt marsh ecosystems. Non-native plants and animals can disrupt the ecological balance of salt marshes, outcompeting native species and altering habitat structure. For example, invasive plants such as *Phragmites australis* (common reed) can dominate salt marshes, reducing biodiversity and altering nutrient cycling. Similarly, invasive crabs and other herbivores can damage native vegetation, hindering restoration efforts.

Effective management of invasive species requires a combination of prevention, control, and restoration strategies. Prevention is the first line of defense and involves measures to reduce the introduction and spread of invasive species. This includes monitoring pathways of introduction, such as ballast water from ships or the intentional planting of non-native species, and implementing policies to regulate these activities.

For existing infestations, control measures are necessary to remove or suppress invasive species. Mechanical removal, such as mowing or cutting invasive plants, is a common approach, but it must be done carefully to avoid damaging native vegetation. Chemical control, using herbicides or pesticides, can be effective for managing invasive plants or animals but must be used sparingly and with consideration for non-target species and overall ecosystem health.

Biological control, which involves introducing natural predators or pathogens to target invasive species, is another option. For example, some restoration projects have successfully used native herbivores to control invasive plants. However, biological control must be carefully researched and monitored to avoid unintended consequences, such as the introduction of new invasive species or disruption to non-target populations.

Once invasive species are removed or suppressed, restoration efforts should focus on re-establishing native vegetation and promoting ecological resilience. Planting native species helps restore the natural structure and function of the salt marsh, creating a competitive advantage against potential reinvasions. Additionally, fostering biodiversity through habitat restoration can strengthen ecosystem resilience, making it more difficult for invasive species to gain a foothold.

Integrated Approaches to Address Challenges

Addressing sea-level rise and invasive species in salt marsh restoration requires integrated approaches that consider the interconnectedness of these challenges. For instance, sediment augmentation not only helps marshes adapt to sea-level rise but also improves habitat conditions for native vegetation, reducing the competitive edge of invasive plants. Similarly, managing invasive species can enhance sediment stability and nutrient cycling, supporting the long-term resilience of marsh ecosystems.

Community engagement and stakeholder collaboration are critical components of successful restoration. Local communities, policymakers, and conservation organizations must work together to implement adaptive management strategies that address both sea-level rise and invasive species. Public education and outreach can also increase awareness of the threats facing salt marshes and the importance of their conservation.

Chapter 5: Wetlands for Coastal Resilience

Wetlands are among the most productive and ecologically significant ecosystems on the planet, playing a crucial role in supporting biodiversity, regulating water cycles, and providing essential ecosystem services. In coastal regions, wetlands act as natural buffers against environmental challenges, such as storm surges, coastal erosion, and flooding. Their ability to absorb and store large volumes of water makes them invaluable in enhancing coastal resilience, particularly in the face of climate change and sea-level rise.

This chapter explores the critical role of wetlands in building coastal resilience. It examines their functions in mitigating the impacts of extreme weather events, improving water quality, and supporting diverse habitats. The chapter also highlights restoration techniques and conservation strategies that can enhance the resilience of degraded wetlands. Additionally, it discusses the importance of integrating wetland management into broader coastal planning and climate adaptation frameworks.

By understanding the ecological and protective roles of wetlands, this chapter underscores their value as Nature-Based Solutions for sustainable coastal management and climate resilience.

Wetlands' Contribution to Coastal Resilience

Wetlands are vital ecosystems that play a key role in enhancing coastal resilience. These biologically diverse areas, located where land meets water, are characterized by saturated soils and vegetation adapted to waterlogged conditions. Coastal wetlands, including marshes, swamps, and tidal flats, provide numerous ecological functions and services that protect coastlines, mitigate the effects of natural disasters, and help communities adapt to climate change.

Flood Mitigation and Storm Protection

One of the most important contributions of wetlands to coastal resilience is their ability to mitigate flooding and protect against storm surges. Wetlands act as natural sponges, absorbing and storing large volumes of water during heavy rainfall, high tides, or storm events. By slowing the flow of water and distributing it across their expanse, wetlands reduce the intensity and speed of floodwaters, thereby minimizing damage to downstream areas.

During hurricanes or cyclones, coastal wetlands serve as natural buffers, absorbing wave energy and reducing the height and strength of storm surges before they reach inhabited areas. This protective function is particularly valuable for communities in low-lying coastal regions that are highly vulnerable to extreme weather events. Studies have shown that areas with intact wetlands suffer significantly less damage from storms compared to those without such natural barriers.

Erosion Control and Sediment Stabilization

Wetlands play a critical role in stabilizing coastlines and controlling erosion. The dense vegetation in wetlands, such as grasses, shrubs, and mangroves, anchors sediments and prevents them from being washed away by tides, currents, and waves. This stabilization helps maintain the integrity of coastal landscapes, protecting infrastructure and agricultural land from erosion.

Additionally, wetlands trap and accumulate sediments carried by rivers and tides, contributing to land formation and the maintenance of wetland elevation. This process is particularly important in the face of sea-level rise, as it allows wetlands to adapt by building up their surface and remaining within the intertidal zone where they can continue to function effectively.

Carbon Sequestration and Climate Mitigation

Coastal wetlands are among the most effective ecosystems for sequestering carbon, making them vital in mitigating climate change.

Known as "blue carbon" ecosystems, wetlands capture and store carbon dioxide in their vegetation and soils. The organic-rich sediments in wetlands act as long-term carbon reservoirs, storing significantly more carbon per unit area than terrestrial forests.

By sequestering carbon, wetlands help offset greenhouse gas emissions and contribute to global climate goals. Protecting and restoring these ecosystems not only enhances coastal resilience but also mitigates the broader impacts of climate change by reducing atmospheric carbon concentrations.

Biodiversity Support and Ecosystem Services

Wetlands are biodiversity hotspots, supporting a wide range of plant and animal species. They provide critical habitats for fish, birds, amphibians, and invertebrates, many of which rely on wetlands for feeding, breeding, and shelter. The high biodiversity of wetlands enhances their ecological resilience, allowing them to recover from disturbances and continue providing ecosystem services.

These ecosystems also play a role in supporting adjacent habitats, such as coral reefs, seagrass meadows, and mangroves, through the exchange of nutrients and species. The interconnectedness of wetlands with other coastal ecosystems amplifies their contribution to coastal resilience, creating a network of habitats that collectively enhance ecological stability.

Water Quality Improvement

Wetlands act as natural filters, improving water quality by trapping sediments, nutrients, and pollutants. As water flows through wetlands, it slows down, allowing sediments to settle out and nutrients to be absorbed by vegetation and microbial communities. This process prevents excessive nutrients, such as nitrogen and phosphorus, from reaching coastal waters, reducing the risk of harmful algal blooms and eutrophication.

By improving water quality, wetlands protect the health of marine and coastal ecosystems, which are vital for fisheries, tourism, and recreational activities. This function also supports the resilience of human communities that depend on clean water for their livelihoods and well-being.

Cultural and Economic Contributions

In addition to their ecological functions, wetlands contribute to the resilience of coastal communities by supporting cultural and economic activities. They provide resources such as fish, shellfish, and reeds, which are vital for local economies. Wetlands are also valued for their aesthetic and recreational appeal, attracting tourists and providing opportunities for activities like birdwatching, kayaking, and photography.

The cultural significance of wetlands is evident in many coastal communities, where they are deeply tied to traditions, practices, and heritage. By maintaining the cultural identity and economic stability of these communities, wetlands enhance social resilience and adaptive capacity.

Restoration Approaches for Wetlands (Sediment Addition, Species Reintroduction)

Restoring wetlands is a critical strategy for safeguarding their ecological functions and enhancing coastal resilience. Two widely used restoration approaches are sediment addition and species reintroduction. These techniques address key challenges such as land subsidence, erosion, biodiversity loss, and habitat degradation, helping wetlands recover their ability to protect coastlines, support biodiversity, and provide essential ecosystem services.

Sediment Addition

Sediment addition, also known as sediment augmentation or nourishment, is a restoration technique used to address the loss of elevation and soil degradation in wetlands. This approach involves the deliberate placement of sediment onto the wetland surface to counteract subsidence, sea-level rise, and erosion. By restoring elevation and improving soil conditions, sediment addition enhances the capacity of wetlands to function as intertidal ecosystems.

1. The Need for Sediment Addition

Wetlands naturally accumulate sediment through tidal flows and riverine processes. However, human activities such as dam construction, land reclamation, and channel dredging disrupt sediment supply, leading to a loss of wetland elevation. Sea-level rise exacerbates this problem, causing wetlands to become inundated and reducing their ability to support vegetation and wildlife.

2. Implementation Process

The sediment addition process begins with sourcing suitable sediment that matches the composition and grain size of the target wetland. Potential sediment sources include dredged materials from nearby waterways, natural deposits, or sediments produced during coastal construction projects. The sediment must be free of contaminants to avoid harming wetland ecosystems.

Once the sediment is sourced, it is transported to the restoration site using barges, pipelines, or trucks. The sediment is then spread evenly across the wetland surface using techniques such as thin-layer placement or hydraulic spraying. These methods ensure that the sediment is applied at the appropriate depth to support vegetation growth without causing excessive disturbance to existing ecosystems.

3. Benefits of Sediment Addition

Sediment addition restores wetland elevation, allowing vegetation to thrive in the intertidal zone. This improves the wetland's ability to trap additional sediment naturally, creating a positive feedback loop that sustains long-term elevation. The added sediment also enhances soil quality by increasing organic matter and nutrient availability, fostering plant growth and habitat development.

In addition, sediment addition increases the wetland's resilience to sea-level rise and storm surges. By raising the wetland surface, this technique helps wetlands maintain their role as natural buffers, protecting coastal areas from flooding and erosion.

4. Challenges and Considerations

While sediment addition is effective, it presents challenges such as high costs and logistical complexity. Sourcing and transporting large quantities of sediment can be resource-intensive, especially for large-scale projects. Furthermore, sediment placement must be carefully managed to avoid disrupting nearby ecosystems, such as seagrass beds or coral reefs.

Monitoring and adaptive management are essential to ensure the success of sediment addition projects. Regular assessments of sediment stability, vegetation recovery, and hydrological conditions help identify potential issues and guide adjustments to the restoration strategy.

Species Reintroduction

Species reintroduction is another key approach to wetland restoration, focusing on re-establishing native plants and animals that have been lost due to habitat degradation, pollution, or overexploitation. This technique enhances biodiversity, restores ecological functions, and strengthens the resilience of wetland ecosystems.

1. The Importance of Native Species

Native plant and animal species are integral to the structure and function of wetlands. Vegetation stabilizes sediments, provides food and habitat for wildlife, and regulates water quality. Similarly, animals such as birds, fish, and invertebrates play vital roles in nutrient cycling, seed dispersal, and maintaining ecological balance.

When native species are lost or populations decline, wetlands become less resilient to environmental changes and disturbances. Reintroducing these species is essential for restoring the ecological integrity of degraded wetlands.

2. Plant Reintroduction

Plant reintroduction involves selecting native species that are well-adapted to local environmental conditions. Common wetland plants used in restoration include cordgrass (*Spartina*), cattails (*Typha*), and bulrushes (*Schoenoplectus*). These species are chosen for their ability to stabilize sediments, tolerate salinity, and support diverse wildlife.

The process begins with propagating plants in nurseries or collecting seeds and cuttings from healthy wetland populations. Once ready, these plants are transplanted to the restoration site using techniques such as hand planting, broadcasting seeds, or deploying pre-grown mats of vegetation. Proper spacing and density are critical to ensure successful establishment and minimize competition among plants.

3. Animal Reintroduction

Reintroducing animal species involves restoring populations of wetland-dependent wildlife, such as fish, amphibians, waterfowl, and invertebrates. This process often requires habitat enhancement to create suitable conditions for these species. For example, restoring water flow, planting vegetation, and constructing nesting sites can encourage the return of migratory birds or fish populations.

In some cases, captive breeding programs are used to reintroduce threatened or endangered species to restored wetlands. These programs involve breeding animals in controlled environments and releasing them into the wild once conditions are favorable. Monitoring and managing the reintroduced populations are essential to ensure their survival and integration into the ecosystem.

4. Benefits of Species Reintroduction

Reintroducing native species restores the ecological functions of wetlands, such as nutrient cycling, food web dynamics, and habitat provision. Vegetation reintroduction stabilizes sediments, reduces erosion, and enhances carbon sequestration, while animal reintroduction supports biodiversity and improves ecosystem resilience.

Species reintroduction also benefits human communities by increasing the availability of resources such as fish and waterfowl, supporting traditional practices, and enhancing recreational opportunities.

5. Challenges and Limitations

Species reintroduction faces challenges such as habitat degradation, competition from invasive species, and climate change. For example, reintroduced plants and animals may struggle to establish if water quality is poor or if invasive species outcompete them. Addressing these challenges requires a comprehensive restoration plan that includes habitat improvement, invasive species management, and ongoing monitoring.

Combining Approaches for Effective Restoration

In many cases, sediment addition and species reintroduction are used together to achieve comprehensive wetland restoration. Sediment addition creates the physical conditions needed for vegetation establishment, while species reintroduction restores the ecological functions of the wetland. This integrated approach maximizes the benefits of restoration and ensures the long-term sustainability of wetland ecosystems.

Urban Integration of Wetland Ecosystems

Urban areas often develop in proximity to wetlands, given their historical role in providing water, resources, and flood protection. However, urbanization has frequently led to the degradation and loss of these ecosystems due to land reclamation, pollution, and infrastructure development. Integrating wetland ecosystems into urban environments offers a sustainable way to enhance biodiversity, improve climate resilience, and provide ecosystem services while supporting urban growth. This section explores how urban integration of wetlands can be achieved and highlights the benefits and challenges of such initiatives.

The Role of Wetlands in Urban Areas

Wetlands serve multiple functions that are crucial for urban resilience and sustainability. They act as natural flood control systems by absorbing and storing stormwater, reducing the risk of flooding during heavy rainfall. Wetlands also improve water quality by filtering pollutants, sediments, and nutrients from urban runoff, ensuring cleaner water for both human use and downstream ecosystems.

Additionally, urban wetlands provide green spaces that enhance the quality of life for city residents. These areas offer recreational opportunities, such as walking, birdwatching, and kayaking, and contribute to physical and mental well-being. Wetlands also act as carbon sinks, sequestering greenhouse gases and mitigating the impacts of urban heat islands, making them valuable for urban climate adaptation.

Strategies for Integrating Wetlands into Urban Planning

1. Restoring and Protecting Existing Wetlands

The first step in urban wetland integration is the protection and restoration of existing wetlands. This involves identifying remaining wetlands in urban areas and implementing measures to prevent further degradation. Restoration efforts may include removing invasive species, improving water flow, and reintroducing native vegetation. Legal and regulatory frameworks, such as zoning laws and protected area designations, can ensure the long-term preservation of urban wetlands.

2. Designing Constructed Wetlands

In areas where natural wetlands have been lost, constructed wetlands can serve as a functional alternative. These engineered systems mimic the ecological processes of natural wetlands and are designed to manage stormwater, improve water quality, and support biodiversity. Constructed wetlands can be integrated into urban infrastructure, such as parks, retention basins, and wastewater treatment facilities, providing ecological benefits alongside practical urban functions.

3. Incorporating Wetlands into Urban Green Networks

Wetlands can be included as part of a broader network of green infrastructure in cities. These networks connect wetlands with parks, green roofs, and urban forests, creating corridors that enhance biodiversity and ecological connectivity. By linking wetlands with other natural and semi-natural areas, cities can amplify the benefits of urban green spaces and support the movement of wildlife and plant species.

4. Community Engagement and Education

Successful integration of wetlands into urban environments requires the involvement of local communities. Public engagement initiatives, such as educational programs, citizen science projects, and community-led restoration activities, can foster a sense of ownership and stewardship. Educating residents about the importance of wetlands helps build support for their protection and encourages sustainable practices that reduce negative impacts on these ecosystems.

5. Policy Integration and Incentives

Urban wetland integration must be supported by policy frameworks that promote sustainable urban planning and development. Policies that incentivize the preservation and restoration of wetlands, such as tax breaks or grants for green infrastructure projects, can encourage developers and municipalities to prioritize wetland conservation. Additionally, integrating wetland considerations into urban master plans and climate adaptation strategies ensures their inclusion in long-term urban development goals.

Benefits of Urban Wetland Integration

Urban integration of wetlands provides multiple benefits that enhance the sustainability and resilience of cities. These include:

• **Flood Risk Reduction**: Wetlands absorb and retain stormwater, reducing the severity of flooding in urban areas.

• **Water Quality Improvement**: Wetlands filter urban runoff, improving the quality of water entering rivers, lakes, and groundwater systems.

• **Biodiversity Support**: Urban wetlands provide habitat for a variety of species, contributing to urban biodiversity and ecological balance.

• **Climate Mitigation**: Wetlands sequester carbon and reduce the effects of urban heat islands, helping cities adapt to climate change.

• **Recreational and Aesthetic Value**: Wetlands enhance urban landscapes, offering recreational opportunities and improving residents' quality of life.

Challenges in Urban Wetland Integration

Despite their benefits, integrating wetlands into urban environments poses several challenges. Urban development pressures often prioritize economic growth over ecological preservation, leading to conflicts between wetland conservation and land use. Additionally, wetlands in urban areas are vulnerable to pollution from runoff, waste, and industrial discharges, which can degrade their ecological functions.

Another challenge is balancing the needs of urban populations with wetland conservation. High population densities and competing demands for space can make it difficult to allocate land for wetland restoration or protection. Effective urban wetland integration requires addressing these challenges through innovative planning, robust policies, and strong community involvement.

Chapter 6: Dunes and Beaches for Erosion Control

Coastal dunes and beaches are among the first lines of defense against coastal erosion, storm surges, and rising sea levels. These dynamic systems play a vital role in stabilizing shorelines, protecting inland areas, and supporting diverse ecosystems. Composed of sand and shaped by wind, waves, and vegetation, dunes and beaches naturally absorb wave energy, reduce erosion, and provide critical habitat for plants and animals.

This chapter examines the importance of dunes and beaches in coastal erosion control, focusing on their ecological functions and protective capabilities. It explores the processes that sustain these systems, including sediment transport and vegetation growth, and highlights the threats posed by human activities and climate change. The chapter also discusses restoration and management strategies, such as dune stabilization, beach nourishment, and vegetation planting, that enhance their resilience and effectiveness.

By understanding the role of dunes and beaches as Nature-Based Solutions for erosion control, this chapter emphasizes their value in sustainable coastal management and climate adaptation efforts.

Importance of Dunes and Beaches in Coastal Systems

Dunes and beaches are integral components of coastal systems, providing a range of ecological, social, and protective functions. These natural landforms are shaped by the interplay of wind, waves, and sediment, creating dynamic environments that serve as buffers against coastal hazards, habitats for wildlife, and recreational spaces for human communities. Despite their importance, dunes and beaches are under increasing pressure from climate change, human activities, and rising sea levels, making their conservation and management critical.

Natural Barriers Against Erosion and Flooding

One of the primary roles of dunes and beaches is their function as natural barriers against coastal erosion and flooding. Beaches dissipate wave energy as waves approach the shore, reducing the impact of strong tides and storm surges. This process helps protect inland areas from damage caused by high-energy waves and prevents the loss of valuable coastal land.

Dunes, formed by windblown sand stabilized by vegetation, act as secondary defenses. They provide an elevated buffer that absorbs and deflects wave energy during storms, reducing the risk of flooding in low-lying areas. By trapping sand and maintaining elevation, dunes also help mitigate the effects of sea-level rise, ensuring long-term shoreline stability.

Habitat Provision and Biodiversity Support

Dunes and beaches are biodiversity hotspots, supporting a variety of plant and animal species that have adapted to the harsh coastal environment. Beaches provide nesting grounds for marine species such as sea turtles, which rely on sandy shores to lay their eggs. Shorebirds, including plovers and sandpipers, forage along the intertidal zone, while crabs and other invertebrates inhabit the beach ecosystem.

Dunes support a unique assemblage of vegetation, such as grasses and shrubs, that are tolerant of salt spray, wind, and shifting sands. This vegetation not only stabilizes the dunes but also provides habitat for insects, small mammals, and birds. The interconnectedness of these species and their reliance on dune and beach ecosystems highlight the importance of preserving these habitats for biodiversity conservation.

Sediment Transport and Coastal Dynamics

Dunes and beaches play a critical role in the natural sediment transport processes that shape coastal systems. Beaches act as reservoirs of sand, storing and redistributing sediment through wave action and tidal flows. During periods of high energy, such as storms, sand may be eroded from the beach and deposited offshore. In calmer conditions, this sand is gradually returned to the shoreline, maintaining the beach's structure.

Dunes contribute to sediment transport by capturing windblown sand and storing it within their vegetation. This trapped sand can be released back to the beach system during erosion events, ensuring a continuous supply of sediment to the coastal zone. These processes highlight the dynamic nature of dunes and beaches and their importance in maintaining the balance of coastal systems.

Carbon Sequestration and Climate Mitigation

Although often overlooked, dunes and beaches contribute to climate regulation through carbon sequestration. Coastal dune vegetation, such as grasses and shrubs, absorbs carbon dioxide from the atmosphere and stores it in its biomass. Additionally, the organic material trapped in the sand contributes to soil carbon storage.

While their carbon storage capacity is smaller compared to other coastal ecosystems like mangroves and seagrass meadows, dunes and beaches still play a role in mitigating climate change. Protecting and restoring these ecosystems can enhance their carbon sequestration potential and contribute to global efforts to reduce greenhouse gas concentrations.

Recreational and Economic Value

Dunes and beaches are among the most valued natural features for recreation and tourism, drawing millions of visitors annually. They provide opportunities for activities such as swimming, sunbathing, fishing, and wildlife observation, contributing to the physical and mental well-being of local communities and tourists.

The economic value of beaches and dunes extends beyond tourism. Healthy beaches protect infrastructure, such as roads and buildings, from storm damage, reducing repair and maintenance costs. Dunes, by buffering inland areas from flooding, safeguard agricultural land and freshwater resources, supporting local economies. The combined ecological and economic benefits of these systems underscore their importance to human well-being.

Vulnerability and the Need for Conservation

Despite their importance, dunes and beaches are highly vulnerable to degradation. Climate change exacerbates erosion and sea-level rise, threatening the stability of these landforms. Human activities, such as coastal development, sand mining, and recreational overuse, further disrupt their natural processes and reduce their capacity to function as protective barriers.

Effective conservation and management are essential to address these challenges. Strategies such as beach nourishment, dune stabilization, and sustainable land-use planning can help maintain the integrity of dunes and beaches. Engaging local communities and stakeholders in conservation efforts ensures long-term protection and promotes awareness of the value of these ecosystems.

Nature-Based Solutions Techniques for Dunes and Beaches (Vegetation Planting, Sand Fencing, Nourishment)

NbS for dunes and beaches focus on harnessing natural processes to enhance coastal resilience, protect against erosion, and support biodiversity. Three key techniques—vegetation planting, sand fencing, and beach nourishment—are widely used to restore and stabilize these dynamic coastal systems. By integrating these approaches, coastal managers can enhance the ecological and protective functions of dunes and beaches while promoting sustainability.

Vegetation Planting

Vegetation planting is a fundamental NbS technique for stabilizing dunes and enhancing their resilience to erosion. Coastal dune vegetation, such as grasses, shrubs, and groundcover plants, plays a critical role in trapping and stabilizing sand, reducing wind erosion, and promoting dune growth.

1. Importance of Vegetation in Dune Stabilization

Dune vegetation acts as a natural barrier against wind and water forces. The dense network of roots binds sand particles together, preventing erosion and maintaining the structural integrity of dunes. Above-ground vegetation reduces wind speed at the surface, encouraging the deposition of sand and aiding in dune formation. Species such as marram grass (*Ammophila arenaria*), beachgrass (*Panicum amarum*), and sea oats (*Uniola paniculata*) are commonly used for their ability to thrive in sandy, saline conditions.

2. Implementation Process

Vegetation planting begins with site assessment to determine the appropriate plant species and planting density based on local environmental conditions, such as wind patterns, salinity levels, and tidal influences. Seeds, seedlings, or mature plants are planted in rows or clusters to maximize sand-trapping efficiency.

Techniques like using biodegradable mats or netting can help stabilize the sand during the initial growth phase. Additionally, irrigation and fertilization may be used in some cases to ensure successful establishment, although these should be minimized to avoid long-term dependency.

3. Benefits and Challenges

Vegetation planting provides long-term stability and promotes natural dune growth, enhancing coastal resilience. It also supports biodiversity by creating habitats for wildlife, including nesting birds and insects. However, this technique can take time to achieve noticeable results, and initial survival rates may be low in harsh coastal environments. Ongoing maintenance, such as invasive species management and replanting, is essential to ensure success.

Sand Fencing

Sand fencing is a simple yet effective technique for promoting dune growth and stabilization by encouraging the natural accumulation of sand. Sand fences are typically made of wooden slats, biodegradable materials, or mesh and are installed in specific patterns to trap windblown sand and protect vulnerable areas.

1. Function and Design

Sand fences work by reducing wind velocity near the ground, causing sand particles to settle and accumulate around the fence. Over time, this accumulation leads to the formation or restoration of dunes. Fences are often installed in a zigzag or checkerboard pattern to maximize their effectiveness in trapping sand.

The height, spacing, and material of sand fences are critical design considerations. Low fences are generally more effective for promoting gradual sand accumulation, while taller fences may be used to protect existing dunes from erosion.

2. Placement and Installation

Sand fences are typically placed along the seaward edge of dunes or in areas where new dunes are being established. They can also be used to protect newly planted vegetation by reducing wind and sand movement. Installation involves anchoring the fences securely into the sand to withstand high winds and wave activity.

3. Benefits and Challenges

Sand fencing is cost-effective and easy to implement, making it a popular choice for dune restoration projects. It promotes natural processes, reducing the need for extensive human intervention. However, sand fences require regular maintenance, as they can be damaged by storms or buried under excessive sand accumulation. Additionally, improper placement can disrupt natural sediment transport and impact adjacent areas.

Beach Nourishment

Beach nourishment involves the addition of sand to eroded beaches to restore their width, elevation, and protective functions. This technique not only enhances the physical stability of beaches but also provides a buffer against coastal erosion and storm surges.

1. Purpose and Process

The primary goal of beach nourishment is to replenish sand lost to erosion, thereby maintaining the beach's ability to dissipate wave energy and protect inland areas. Sand for nourishment is typically sourced from offshore dredging sites, riverbeds, or terrestrial quarries. It is transported to the target site and distributed along the beach using bulldozers, pipelines, or barges.

The added sand is carefully graded to match the natural slope and profile of the beach, ensuring seamless integration with the existing shoreline. To maximize effectiveness, nourishment projects are often timed to avoid storm seasons or nesting periods for wildlife.

2. Environmental and Ecological Considerations

Selecting appropriate sand for nourishment is critical to minimizing ecological impacts. The grain size, composition, and color of the added sand should match the natural characteristics of the beach to avoid altering habitat conditions. Monitoring is essential to assess the impact on benthic organisms and ensure that sedimentation does not harm nearby ecosystems, such as coral reefs or seagrass meadows.

3. Benefits and Challenges

Beach nourishment enhances coastal protection, improves recreational opportunities, and supports tourism-dependent economies. It also provides immediate results, making it a practical solution for addressing severe erosion. However, the technique is resource-intensive and requires significant financial investment. Nourished beaches are not permanent solutions and may require periodic replenishment as erosion continues.

Integrating NbS Techniques

In many coastal restoration projects, vegetation planting, sand fencing, and beach nourishment are used in combination to maximize their benefits. For example, sand fencing can be installed to promote initial dune formation, followed by vegetation planting to stabilize the accumulated sand. Beach nourishment may be employed simultaneously to replenish eroded areas and provide a stable foundation for these interventions.

Integrating these techniques also enhances their effectiveness by addressing multiple aspects of dune and beach dynamics. For instance, while vegetation planting focuses on long-term stabilization, sand fencing and beach nourishment provide immediate erosion control and protection.

Challenges in Implementing NbS Techniques

While NbS techniques offer sustainable solutions for dune and beach restoration, their implementation is not without challenges. High costs, logistical constraints, and potential ecological impacts can hinder large-scale projects. Additionally, climate change introduces uncertainties, such as increased storm intensity and rising sea levels, which may reduce the longevity of these interventions.

Public awareness and stakeholder engagement are critical for overcoming these challenges. Educating local communities about the importance of dunes and beaches and involving them in restoration efforts can foster long-term stewardship and support for NbS initiatives.

Managing Tourism and Balancing Recreation with Conservation

Coastal dunes and beaches are some of the most popular destinations for recreation and tourism, drawing millions of visitors annually. These areas provide opportunities for relaxation, outdoor activities, and wildlife observation, making them economically and culturally significant. However, intensive tourism and recreational use can threaten the ecological integrity of these natural systems, leading to erosion, habitat degradation, and pollution. Managing tourism and balancing recreation with conservation are essential to protect dunes and beaches while allowing people to enjoy their benefits.

The Impacts of Tourism and Recreation

Tourism and recreational activities can have significant ecological and environmental impacts on dunes and beaches. Heavy foot traffic and off-road vehicles disturb vegetation, compact the sand, and destabilize dunes, increasing the risk of erosion. Trampling of dune vegetation reduces its ability to trap sand, weakening the natural processes that maintain these systems.

Littering and pollution from tourism also degrade the quality of coastal ecosystems. Plastics, food waste, and other debris not only harm wildlife but also disrupt natural processes such as sediment transport. Water quality can be affected by runoff from nearby tourism infrastructure, further impacting marine and coastal biodiversity.

Overcrowding during peak tourism seasons exacerbates these issues, concentrating environmental pressures in specific areas. Without proper management, these impacts can lead to the long-term degradation of dunes and beaches, reducing their ability to provide ecosystem services and diminishing their appeal as tourist destinations.

Strategies for Balancing Recreation and Conservation

1. Zoning and Access Management

Implementing zoning regulations is one of the most effective ways to balance tourism and conservation. By designating specific areas for recreational use, such as walking paths, picnic zones, and vehicle-accessible beaches, sensitive habitats like dunes and nesting areas can be protected. Restricted access zones can be established to prevent human disturbance in ecologically critical areas.

Boardwalks and raised pathways can be constructed to guide visitors over dunes without damaging vegetation or compacting the sand. These structures minimize direct human impact while allowing tourists to enjoy the natural beauty of the area.

2. Education and Awareness Programs

Public education is critical for fostering responsible tourism and recreation. Informative signage, visitor centers, and guided tours can raise awareness about the ecological importance of dunes and beaches and the need for conservation. Programs that highlight the impacts of littering, trampling, and off-road driving can encourage tourists to adopt sustainable behaviors.

Community engagement initiatives, such as beach cleanups and citizen science projects, can also promote a sense of stewardship among local residents and visitors. These activities help build a culture of conservation that benefits both the environment and the tourism industry.

3. Sustainable Infrastructure Development

Tourism infrastructure, such as hotels, restaurants, and parking facilities, should be designed with sustainability in mind. Coastal developments should be located away from sensitive habitats to reduce their ecological footprint. Low-impact construction techniques, renewable energy use, and efficient waste management systems can further minimize environmental impacts.

Seasonal restrictions on tourism infrastructure, such as limiting operations during nesting periods for wildlife, can protect vulnerable species and habitats. For example, some coastal areas implement temporary beach closures to safeguard sea turtle nesting sites.

4. Carrying Capacity Assessments

Determining the carrying capacity of dunes and beaches helps prevent overuse and overcrowding. Carrying capacity assessments evaluate the number of visitors an area can accommodate without causing significant environmental harm. Based on these assessments, visitor limits can be set, and permits or timed entry systems can be introduced to manage the flow of tourists.

Dynamic management approaches, such as adjusting visitor limits based on seasonal conditions or ecosystem health, allow for more flexible and effective conservation efforts.

Benefits of Balancing Recreation and Conservation

Balancing recreation with conservation offers multiple benefits for both the environment and local communities. Healthy dunes and beaches maintain their ecological functions, such as erosion control, biodiversity support, and carbon sequestration, ensuring long-term sustainability. These preserved ecosystems also enhance the aesthetic and recreational value of coastal areas, attracting environmentally conscious tourists and supporting eco-tourism initiatives.

Local economies benefit from sustainable tourism practices through job creation and revenue generation, while reduced environmental degradation lowers the costs of restoration and management. Engaging communities in conservation efforts strengthens their connection to the area and fosters a shared responsibility for its protection.

Challenges in Managing Tourism and Conservation

Managing tourism while protecting dunes and beaches involves several challenges. Conflicts may arise between conservation goals and economic interests, particularly in areas heavily reliant on tourism revenue. Local authorities and businesses may prioritize short-term profits over long-term sustainability, leading to overdevelopment and habitat destruction.

Enforcing regulations and maintaining infrastructure can be resource-intensive, requiring financial and logistical support. Limited funding for conservation programs may hinder the implementation of effective management strategies.

Climate change adds another layer of complexity, as rising sea levels, increased storm intensity, and changing weather patterns exacerbate the vulnerability of dunes and beaches. Adaptive management approaches are necessary to address these challenges while maintaining a balance between human use and ecological preservation.

Chapter 7: Living Shorelines for Coastal Adaptation

Living shorelines are innovative and sustainable approaches to managing coastal zones, offering natural resilience against erosion, flooding, and sea-level rise. Unlike traditional hard engineering solutions such as seawalls and bulkheads, living shorelines utilize natural elements, including plants, oyster reefs, and other biological structures, to stabilize coastlines while maintaining ecological functions. These solutions blend human needs with environmental preservation, creating adaptable systems that benefit both people and nature.

This chapter explores the concept of living shorelines as a Nature-Based Solution for coastal adaptation. It examines their ecological, protective, and social benefits, emphasizing how they enhance biodiversity, reduce erosion, and support climate resilience. The chapter also discusses design considerations, implementation techniques, and the challenges associated with adopting living shorelines. By understanding the potential of these systems, coastal planners and policymakers can integrate living shorelines into broader strategies for sustainable coastal management.

Definition and Benefits of Living Shorelines

Living shorelines are an innovative approach to coastal management that integrates natural elements with human-designed structures to protect shorelines from erosion, flooding, and other coastal hazards. Unlike traditional hard infrastructure such as seawalls and bulkheads, living shorelines prioritize the use of natural habitats, including marshes, mangroves, dunes, and oyster reefs, to enhance ecological resilience and maintain ecosystem functions. By blending natural and engineered components, living shorelines provide sustainable solutions to coastal challenges while supporting biodiversity and offering numerous social and economic benefits.

Definition of Living Shorelines

Living shorelines are coastal stabilization strategies that use a combination of native vegetation, natural materials, and sometimes low-impact engineered structures to protect and restore shorelines. These systems are designed to mimic the natural processes of coastal ecosystems, such as sediment trapping, wave attenuation, and habitat provision, while reducing the impacts of human activities and climate change.

A typical living shoreline may include components like salt marsh vegetation, submerged aquatic plants, sand dunes, and oyster reefs. In some cases, biodegradable materials such as coconut fiber mats or natural fiber logs are used to stabilize the shoreline during the initial establishment phase. These features work together to create a dynamic and adaptable system that can respond to changing environmental conditions over time.

Ecological Benefits

1. Habitat Creation and Biodiversity Support

One of the most significant benefits of living shorelines is their ability to create and restore habitats for a wide variety of species. By incorporating natural elements, these systems provide critical habitats for fish, crustaceans, birds, and other wildlife. For example, marsh vegetation supports juvenile fish and invertebrates, while oyster reefs offer shelter and feeding grounds for marine organisms.

Living shorelines also contribute to ecological connectivity, linking coastal habitats such as wetlands, seagrass meadows, and coral reefs. This connectivity supports migration and breeding cycles, enhancing the overall health and resilience of coastal ecosystems.

2. Erosion Control and Sediment Stabilization

Living shorelines reduce erosion by dissipating wave energy and stabilizing sediments. Vegetation, such as marsh grasses and mangroves, anchors sediments with their root systems, preventing shoreline retreat. Oyster reefs and other natural structures act as physical barriers, reducing wave impact and promoting sediment deposition. Over time, these processes contribute to the growth and stability of the shoreline.

3. Water Quality Improvement

Many components of living shorelines, such as marsh vegetation and oyster reefs, play a role in filtering pollutants and improving water quality. Vegetation absorbs excess nutrients, such as nitrogen and phosphorus, from runoff, preventing eutrophication and harmful algal blooms. Oyster reefs filter large volumes of water, removing suspended particles and pollutants, which enhances the clarity and health of coastal waters.

Protective Benefits

1. Wave Attenuation and Flood Mitigation

Living shorelines provide natural protection against storm surges and wave action, reducing the impact of flooding on coastal communities. Vegetation absorbs and dissipates wave energy, while natural barriers such as reefs and dunes act as buffers that protect inland areas. Unlike hard infrastructure, which often reflects wave energy and exacerbates erosion in adjacent areas, living shorelines absorb and manage wave forces, providing more sustainable protection.

2. Adaptability to Sea-Level Rise

Unlike static hard infrastructure, living shorelines are dynamic and adaptable. They can grow and evolve over time, allowing them to adjust to rising sea levels and other environmental changes. For example, marshes and mangroves can accumulate sediments and organic matter, gradually increasing their elevation to keep pace with sea-level rise. This adaptability makes living shorelines a long-term solution for coastal resilience.

Social and Economic Benefits

1. Cost-Effectiveness and Longevity

While the initial costs of implementing a living shoreline may be similar to or slightly higher than traditional infrastructure, the long-term benefits often outweigh these expenses. Living shorelines require less maintenance and repair compared to hard structures, which can deteriorate over time due to wave impacts and corrosion. Additionally, the ecosystem services provided by living shorelines, such as carbon sequestration and fisheries support, generate long-term economic value.

2. Aesthetic and Recreational Value

Living shorelines enhance the visual appeal of coastal areas by creating natural, green spaces that blend seamlessly with the environment. These areas provide recreational opportunities, such as birdwatching, kayaking, and fishing, which contribute to the well-being of local communities and attract eco-tourism. The aesthetic and recreational value of living shorelines fosters public support for their implementation and maintenance.

3. Community Engagement and Education

The development of living shorelines often involves community participation in planning, restoration, and monitoring efforts. These projects provide opportunities for environmental education and awareness, fostering a sense of stewardship among local residents. Engaged communities are more likely to support conservation initiatives and adopt sustainable practices, contributing to the long-term success of living shoreline projects.

Techniques for Creating Living Shorelines (Vegetation, Oyster Reefs)

Creating living shorelines involves the application of nature-based techniques that stabilize coastlines while preserving and enhancing their ecological functions. Two of the most widely used approaches are vegetation-based solutions and the incorporation of oyster reefs. These techniques work individually or in combination to reduce erosion, protect against storm surges, and support biodiversity. This section explores the processes, benefits, and considerations for using vegetation and oyster reefs in living shoreline projects.

Vegetation-Based Solutions

Using native vegetation is a cornerstone technique in creating living shorelines. Plants such as marsh grasses, mangroves, and other salt-tolerant species play a vital role in stabilizing sediments, absorbing wave energy, and enhancing habitat complexity.

1. Role of Vegetation in Living Shorelines

Vegetation is a natural barrier that helps maintain shoreline integrity. The roots of marsh plants, such as *Spartina alterniflora* (smooth cordgrass) and *Juncus roemerianus* (black needlerush), bind sediments and prevent erosion caused by waves and tidal currents. Above-ground plant structures reduce wind and wave energy, promoting sediment deposition and protecting inland areas from flooding.

2. Implementation Process

The establishment of vegetation in living shorelines typically involves site assessment, species selection, and planting.

• **Site Assessment**: Analyzing factors such as salinity, tidal range, sediment type, and wave exposure is essential to select the appropriate plant species and ensure long-term success.

• **Species Selection**: Native plants adapted to local conditions are chosen for their ability to withstand coastal dynamics. For instance, salt marsh grasses are ideal for low-energy environments, while mangroves are suited for tropical regions with higher wave energy.

• **Planting Techniques**: Seeds, seedlings, or mature plants can be used. Planting is often done in rows or clusters to maximize sediment stabilization and encourage natural expansion. Biodegradable mats or erosion control fabrics are sometimes installed to provide initial support for young plants.

3. Benefits of Vegetation-Based Solutions

Vegetation enhances biodiversity by creating habitats for fish, birds, and invertebrates. It improves water quality by filtering pollutants and excess nutrients, reducing the risk of eutrophication. Additionally, vegetation can adapt and grow with changing environmental conditions, such as sea-level rise, making it a resilient component of living shorelines.

4. Challenges and Maintenance

The success of vegetation-based solutions depends on proper site selection and ongoing maintenance. Factors such as strong wave action, invasive species, or poor water quality can hinder plant establishment. Regular monitoring and supplemental planting may be necessary to ensure long-term stability.

Oyster Reefs

Oyster reefs are another effective technique for creating living shorelines, offering both structural and ecological benefits. These reefs consist of live oysters, shell material, or artificial structures that mimic natural reefs. Oyster reefs reduce wave energy, stabilize sediments, and enhance habitat complexity.

1. Role of Oyster Reefs in Living Shorelines

Oyster reefs serve as natural breakwaters, absorbing and dissipating wave energy before it reaches the shoreline. This function reduces erosion and allows sediment to settle, supporting the growth of vegetation and the formation of stable shorelines. Additionally, oyster reefs provide habitat for marine organisms, enhancing local biodiversity and ecosystem productivity.

2. Implementation Process

The creation of oyster reefs involves several steps, including site selection, material deployment, and reef establishment.

• **Site Selection**: Identifying suitable locations for oyster reef restoration is critical. Factors such as water salinity, tidal flow, substrate type, and existing oyster populations are assessed to ensure optimal conditions for reef growth.

• **Material Deployment**: Oyster reefs can be created using natural shell material, such as oyster shells or limestone, or artificial structures like concrete blocks or biodegradable mesh. These materials are placed on the seafloor to serve as a foundation for oyster larvae (spat) to settle and grow.

• **Reef Establishment**: Oyster larvae are introduced either naturally or through hatchery-reared spat. Over time, these larvae grow into mature oysters, forming dense, interconnected reef structures. In some cases, existing oyster populations are supplemented to accelerate reef formation.

3. Benefits of Oyster Reefs

Oyster reefs provide multiple ecological and protective benefits. They improve water quality by filtering large volumes of water, removing suspended particles, and reducing nutrient levels. A single oyster can filter up to 50 gallons of water per day, enhancing the clarity and health of coastal waters. Oyster reefs also support fisheries by creating habitats for economically important species, such as shrimp, crabs, and fish.

From a structural perspective, oyster reefs reduce wave energy by up to 76%, protecting shorelines from erosion and storm surges. Unlike traditional hard infrastructure, oyster reefs grow and adapt over time, increasing their resilience to environmental changes.

4. Challenges and Maintenance

The establishment of oyster reefs can be affected by environmental conditions, such as poor water quality, disease, or predation. Additionally, the availability of suitable shell material or larvae may limit large-scale restoration efforts. Monitoring and adaptive management are required to address these challenges and ensure the long-term success of oyster reefs.

Integrating Vegetation and Oyster Reefs

In many living shoreline projects, vegetation and oyster reefs are used together to maximize their ecological and protective functions. Oyster reefs act as the first line of defense, reducing wave energy and creating calm conditions that promote sediment deposition and vegetation growth. In turn, vegetation stabilizes sediments and enhances the resilience of the shoreline. This synergistic approach creates a multi-layered defense system that supports biodiversity and adapts to changing conditions.

For example, in low-energy environments, marsh vegetation and oyster reefs can be combined to create a self-sustaining shoreline. In higher-energy areas, additional measures, such as biodegradable breakwaters or sand nourishment, may be incorporated to enhance stability.

Challenges and Considerations for Implementation

Despite their benefits, implementing vegetation and oyster reef techniques faces challenges such as funding constraints, land-use conflicts, and climate change impacts. Public engagement and stakeholder collaboration are critical to overcoming these barriers. Educating communities about the value of living shorelines and involving them in restoration efforts can build support and ensure long-term success.

Additionally, adaptive management practices are essential to address uncertainties, such as changes in sea levels, storm intensity, or water quality. Regular monitoring and data collection can inform adjustments to restoration strategies, ensuring that living shorelines remain effective over time.

Comparison to Traditional Hard Infrastructure

Coastal protection strategies have traditionally relied on hard infrastructure, such as seawalls, bulkheads, and revetments, to safeguard shorelines from erosion, storm surges, and flooding. While these engineered structures are effective in certain contexts, they often come with significant ecological, economic, and social drawbacks. In contrast, living shorelines offer a nature-based alternative that addresses these limitations while providing additional benefits. This section compares living shorelines to traditional hard infrastructure, focusing on their effectiveness, ecological impacts, adaptability, and cost considerations.

Effectiveness in Coastal Protection

Traditional Hard Infrastructure

Hard infrastructure is designed to provide immediate and robust protection against coastal hazards. Structures such as seawalls and bulkheads act as physical barriers, preventing wave energy from reaching the shoreline. In high-energy environments or densely developed areas, hard infrastructure can effectively reduce erosion and protect infrastructure.

However, hard structures often have unintended consequences. By reflecting wave energy rather than dissipating it, they can exacerbate erosion in adjacent areas, a phenomenon known as "end scour." Over time, this can undermine the very structures they are meant to protect, requiring costly repairs or replacements.

Living Shorelines

Living shorelines, in contrast, dissipate wave energy naturally through vegetation, oyster reefs, and other natural features. These systems stabilize sediments, reduce wave impact, and allow for sediment deposition, which contributes to shoreline resilience over time. Unlike hard infrastructure, living shorelines work with natural processes, making them more sustainable and less likely to cause erosion in adjacent areas.

While living shorelines may not provide the same level of immediate protection in high-energy environments as hard infrastructure, their ability to adapt and recover makes them a viable long-term solution for many coastal settings.

Ecological Impacts

Traditional Hard Infrastructure

The construction and presence of hard infrastructure often result in significant ecological disruption. Seawalls and bulkheads replace natural habitats with impervious surfaces, reducing habitat availability for coastal and marine species. These structures can also disrupt sediment transport and alter hydrodynamic conditions, leading to the degradation of nearby ecosystems such as salt marshes, seagrass meadows, and coral reefs.

Additionally, hard infrastructure lacks the capacity to provide ecological benefits, such as water filtration or carbon sequestration, which are essential for maintaining coastal ecosystem health.

Living Shorelines

Living shorelines enhance ecological integrity by preserving and restoring natural habitats. Vegetation and oyster reefs create habitats for a wide range of species, supporting biodiversity and improving ecosystem functions. These systems also contribute to water quality improvement through nutrient uptake and filtration, while their carbon sequestration capacity helps mitigate climate change.

By maintaining ecological connectivity and supporting natural processes, living shorelines offer a more holistic approach to coastal management that benefits both the environment and human communities.

Adaptability and Resilience

Traditional Hard Infrastructure

Hard infrastructure is static by design and lacks the ability to adapt to changing environmental conditions, such as sea-level rise, increased storm intensity, or shifting sediment dynamics. Over time, these changes can render hard structures ineffective, requiring extensive modifications or replacements. Furthermore, hard infrastructure often fails during extreme weather events, leaving coastlines vulnerable to damage.

Living Shorelines

Living shorelines are dynamic and adaptable systems that grow and evolve with environmental changes. For example, marsh vegetation can accumulate sediment and organic matter, gradually increasing elevation to keep pace with sea-level rise. Oyster reefs can expand and strengthen over time as oyster populations grow, enhancing their protective functions.

This adaptability not only makes living shorelines more resilient to long-term changes but also reduces the need for costly interventions, ensuring their effectiveness over time.

Cost Considerations

Traditional Hard Infrastructure

Hard infrastructure projects typically involve high upfront construction costs due to the materials, engineering expertise, and heavy machinery required. Maintenance and repair costs can also be significant, particularly in areas subject to frequent storms or wave action. Over time, the cumulative costs of repairs, replacements, and the environmental damage caused by hard infrastructure can make these solutions economically unsustainable.

Living Shorelines

Living shorelines often have lower initial construction costs, especially when natural materials and local vegetation are used. Although they may require monitoring and maintenance during the establishment phase, the long-term costs are generally lower than those of hard infrastructure. Living shorelines also provide economic value through ecosystem services, such as fisheries support, tourism opportunities, and carbon sequestration, contributing to their overall cost-effectiveness.

Social and Aesthetic Considerations

Traditional Hard Infrastructure

While effective in providing protection, hard infrastructure is often visually unappealing and can reduce coastal areas' aesthetic and recreational value. These structures may restrict public access to beaches and shorelines, limiting outdoor opportunities and negatively impacting coastal communities' quality of life.

Living Shorelines

Living shorelines enhance coastal areas' aesthetic and recreational appeal by creating natural, green spaces that blend seamlessly with the environment. These areas offer opportunities for recreation, such as birdwatching, kayaking, and fishing, and contribute to residents' and visitors' physical and mental well-being. The aesthetic value of living shorelines also fosters community support for their implementation and maintenance.

Chapter 8: Oyster and Shellfish Reefs for Coastal Restoration

Oyster and shellfish reefs are among the most valuable natural structures in coastal ecosystems, providing essential ecological, economic, and protective benefits. These reefs act as natural breakwaters, reducing wave energy, stabilizing sediments, and mitigating shoreline erosion. Additionally, they play a critical role in supporting marine biodiversity, improving water quality, and sustaining fisheries. Despite their importance, oyster and shellfish reefs have experienced significant global declines due to overharvesting, habitat destruction, and pollution.

This chapter explores the potential of oyster and shellfish reefs as Nature-Based Solutions for coastal restoration. It examines their ecological functions, protective capabilities, and contributions to community resilience. The chapter also discusses restoration techniques, challenges, and strategies to integrate these reefs into broader coastal management frameworks. By understanding the role of oyster and shellfish reefs in coastal ecosystems, this chapter highlights their importance in achieving sustainable and resilient coastlines.

Ecological and Protective Benefits of Oyster Reefs

Oyster reefs are vital components of coastal ecosystems, offering significant ecological and protective benefits. These natural structures, formed by dense aggregations of oysters and their shells, provide habitat for diverse marine species, enhance water quality, and protect shorelines from erosion and storm surges. Despite their widespread decline due to overharvesting, pollution, and habitat destruction, oyster reefs remain an essential focus for restoration efforts due to their critical role in supporting both ecosystems and human communities.

Ecological Benefits

1. Habitat Creation and Biodiversity Support

Oyster reefs are biodiversity hotspots, supporting a wide array of marine species. The complex, three-dimensional structure of oyster reefs provides shelter and foraging opportunities for fish, crabs, shrimp, and other invertebrates. Many commercially important species, such as blue crabs, red drum, and shrimp, rely on oyster reefs during various stages of their life cycles.

Oyster reefs also enhance the productivity of adjacent habitats. For example, they are often found in proximity to seagrass meadows and salt marshes, with nutrient exchange and species movement between these ecosystems boosting overall ecological health. The presence of oyster reefs helps maintain the balance and resilience of coastal ecosystems.

2. Water Quality Improvement

Oysters are natural filter feeders, capable of improving water quality by removing suspended particles, algae, and excess nutrients from the water column. A single oyster can filter up to 50 gallons of water per day, reducing turbidity and promoting light penetration, which benefits photosynthetic organisms like seagrasses.

By controlling nutrient levels, oyster reefs also help mitigate the risk of eutrophication and harmful algal blooms. These water quality improvements have cascading benefits for marine ecosystems and human activities, such as fishing and tourism.

3. Carbon Sequestration and Nutrient Cycling

Oyster reefs contribute to carbon sequestration by incorporating carbon into their shells, which are composed of calcium carbonate. This process helps offset greenhouse gas emissions, albeit on a smaller scale compared to other coastal ecosystems like mangroves or seagrasses.

Additionally, oyster reefs play a key role in nutrient cycling. They facilitate the deposition of organic matter onto the seafloor, where microbial processes convert excess nutrients into forms less harmful to the environment. This function supports the overall health and stability of coastal waters.

Protective Benefits

1. Wave Energy Dissipation and Erosion Control

Oyster reefs serve as natural breakwaters, reducing wave energy before it reaches the shoreline. By absorbing and dispersing wave forces, these reefs minimize the impact of storms and high tides on coastal areas. This function not only protects natural habitats but also reduces erosion and the loss of valuable coastal land.

The sediment-stabilizing effects of oyster reefs further enhance their protective role. By trapping and binding sediments, oyster reefs help maintain shoreline elevation and prevent sediment from being washed away. This process is particularly important in areas experiencing sea-level rise or increased storm activity.

2. Storm Surge Mitigation

During extreme weather events, such as hurricanes and cyclones, oyster reefs provide critical protection to coastal communities by mitigating storm surges. The reefs act as physical barriers, reducing the height and energy of incoming waves. This function helps protect infrastructure, reduce flood damage, and safeguard human lives.

Unlike traditional hard infrastructure, such as seawalls, oyster reefs adapt and grow over time, maintaining their protective capabilities even as environmental conditions change. Their ability to self-repair and expand makes them a cost-effective and sustainable solution for long-term coastal resilience.

3. Adaptability to Climate Change

Oyster reefs are dynamic ecosystems that can adapt to environmental changes, such as sea-level rise and shifting sediment patterns. As oyster populations grow, the reefs expand vertically and horizontally, keeping pace with changing conditions. This adaptability ensures that oyster reefs continue to provide ecological and protective benefits in the face of climate change.

Furthermore, oyster reefs contribute to the overall resilience of coastal ecosystems by supporting biodiversity, improving water quality, and maintaining sediment stability. These functions enhance the ability of coastal systems to withstand and recover from environmental stressors.

Economic and Social Impacts

The ecological and protective benefits of oyster reefs extend to human communities, offering economic and social value. Oyster reefs support commercial and recreational fisheries, providing livelihoods for coastal populations. By improving water quality and protecting shorelines, these reefs also enhance the aesthetic and recreational appeal of coastal areas, attracting eco-tourism and boosting local economies.

Community-led oyster reef restoration projects foster a sense of stewardship and environmental awareness, encouraging sustainable practices and stronger connections between people and their natural surroundings. This social dimension adds to the long-term viability and support for oyster reef conservation efforts.

Techniques for Restoring Reefs (Spat-on-Shell, Reef Balls, Breakwaters)

Restoring oyster and shellfish reefs is critical to rehabilitating degraded coastal ecosystems and improving resilience to climate impacts. Techniques such as spat-on-shell, reef balls, and breakwater structures offer scalable and effective approaches to reestablish reef ecosystems while protecting shorelines and enhancing biodiversity. This section discusses each technique's methods, benefits, and challenges.

Spat-on-Shell Technique

Spat-on-shell is one of the most commonly used methods for reef restoration. This technique involves attaching juvenile oysters (spat) to cleaned and sterilized oyster shells, which are then deployed at restoration sites. The goal is to replicate the natural process of oyster settlement and encourage the development of interconnected reefs.

1. Implementation Process

The spat-on-shell technique begins with collecting discarded oyster shells from fisheries, restaurants, or recycling programs. These shells are thoroughly cleaned and treated to eliminate pathogens and organic debris. In controlled hatchery environments, oyster larvae are introduced to tanks containing the prepared shells. The larvae settle on the shells, forming spat-on-shell clusters.

Once the spat have sufficiently attached, the clusters are transported to the designated restoration site. These sites are chosen based on factors such as water salinity, substrate conditions, tidal flow, and proximity to existing oyster populations. The spat-on-shell is deployed on the seabed in targeted patterns, often using biodegradable bags or mesh to hold the clusters in place during initial establishment.

2. Benefits of Spat-on-Shell

• **Reef Formation**: Spat-on-shell allows for the creation of natural reef structures, enhancing habitat complexity.

• **Scalability**: This method can be implemented on small or large scales, depending on project goals and resources.

• **Biodiversity Support**: The reefs provide habitats for marine life, including fish, crabs, and shrimp.

3. Challenges

This technique depends on the availability of clean oyster shells and sufficient larvae. Environmental factors such as water quality, predators, and disease can affect spat survival and reef establishment. Regular monitoring is required to address these issues.

Reef Balls

Reef balls are artificial structures designed to mimic the form and function of natural reefs. Made from concrete or other durable materials, reef balls provide a stable substrate for oyster larvae and serve as protective habitats for marine organisms.

1. Construction and Deployment

Reef balls are constructed using molds that create dome-shaped structures with multiple holes and cavities. These designs maximize surface area for oyster settlement while providing shelter for marine species. Reef balls are often pre-seeded with spat-on-shell or oyster larvae in hatcheries before deployment to accelerate reef formation.

The deployment process involves placing reef balls on the seabed in strategic patterns. They are commonly used in areas where natural reef substrates are unavailable or where wave energy is too high for softer materials. Their weight and durability make them suitable for use in high-energy environments.

2. Benefits of Reef Balls

• **Durability**: Reef balls are designed to withstand strong waves and currents, ensuring long-term stability.

• **Erosion Control**: By reducing wave energy, they protect shorelines from erosion.

• **Habitat Creation**: The cavities and surface texture support diverse marine life.

3. Challenges

Reef balls can be expensive to manufacture and deploy, requiring specialized equipment and expertise. Improper placement can disrupt sediment transport or affect nearby ecosystems. Additionally, their large size and weight may limit their use in certain areas.

Breakwater Structures

Breakwater structures combine hard engineering with ecological restoration to reduce wave energy and promote oyster reef development. These structures, which can be submerged or emergent, serve as physical barriers that protect shorelines while creating favorable conditions for oyster settlement.

1. Types and Construction

Breakwaters are constructed from a range of materials, including rocks, concrete blocks, and biodegradable geotextiles. Submerged breakwaters are placed below the waterline to reduce wave energy without obstructing navigation, while emergent breakwaters rise above the surface to provide additional protection during storms.

These structures are often seeded with oyster larvae or spat-on-shell to encourage reef formation. Textured surfaces or built-in cavities on breakwaters enhance settlement and habitat complexity, allowing them to function as both protective barriers and living ecosystems.

2. Benefits of Breakwaters

• **Wave Attenuation**: Breakwaters significantly reduce wave energy, protecting shorelines and inland areas from storm damage.

• **Dual Functionality**: They combine the benefits of hard infrastructure with ecological restoration.

• **Adaptability**: Breakwaters can be customized to suit various environmental conditions and project goals.

3. Challenges

The construction of breakwaters requires careful planning to avoid unintended impacts on sediment transport and water flow. High costs and potential environmental concerns, such as disruption to existing habitats, must also be considered. Ongoing maintenance is essential to ensure the effectiveness of these structures.

Integrating Techniques

In many restoration projects, spat-on-shell, reef balls, and breakwaters are used in combination to maximize ecological and protective outcomes. For example, breakwaters can be installed to reduce wave energy, creating calmer conditions for spat-on-shell deployment. Reef balls can be placed in high-energy zones to stabilize sediments and provide additional habitat. This integrated approach addresses multiple restoration goals while enhancing the resilience of coastal ecosystems.

Monitoring and Maintenance

All reef restoration techniques require regular monitoring to assess their success and identify areas for improvement. Key metrics include oyster survival rates, reef growth, biodiversity, and water quality. Maintenance activities, such as removing invasive species, repairing damaged structures, or re-seeding oysters, are essential to ensure the long-term sustainability of restored reefs.

Overcoming Challenges (Pollution, Disease, Overharvesting)

Restoring oyster and shellfish reefs is critical for enhancing coastal ecosystems and protecting communities from climate impacts. However, these efforts face significant challenges, including pollution, disease, and overharvesting, which threaten the success of restoration projects and the long-term health of reef ecosystems. Addressing these issues requires targeted strategies that combine science, policy, and community engagement. This section explores the nature of these challenges and outlines solutions for overcoming them.

Pollution

Pollution is one of the most pervasive threats to oyster and shellfish reefs. Runoff from agricultural, urban, and industrial areas carries excess nutrients, sediments, and contaminants into coastal waters, degrading water quality and reef habitats.

1. Impacts on Reefs

Excess nutrients, particularly nitrogen and phosphorus, fuel algal blooms that reduce oxygen levels in the water, creating hypoxic conditions. These "dead zones" can suffocate oysters and other marine life. Sediment runoff smothers reefs, blocking sunlight and hindering larval settlement. Contaminants such as heavy metals and pesticides further stress oyster populations, reducing their growth and reproductive capacity.

2. Solutions

• **Improved Land-Use Practices**: Implementing sustainable agricultural practices, such as buffer zones and reduced fertilizer use, can minimize nutrient runoff. Urban areas can adopt green infrastructure, including rain gardens and permeable pavements, to reduce stormwater pollution.

• **Water Quality Monitoring**: Regular monitoring programs can identify pollution hotspots, enabling targeted interventions to improve water quality.

• **Policy and Regulation**: Stronger enforcement of water quality regulations, such as the Clean Water Act in the United States, can reduce industrial and urban discharges into coastal waters.

By addressing pollution at its source, these measures can create conditions that support oyster reef restoration and ecosystem recovery.

Disease

Disease poses a significant challenge to oyster reef restoration, as pathogens and parasites can devastate oyster populations. Common diseases, such as *Dermo* (caused by *Perkinsus marinus*) and MSX (caused by *Haplosporidium nelsoni*), are particularly problematic in regions with high water temperatures and salinity.

1. Impacts on Reefs

Diseases weaken oysters, reducing their ability to filter water, build reefs, and reproduce. Outbreaks can spread rapidly, especially in densely populated reef systems, threatening restoration efforts and diminishing ecosystem services.

2. Solutions

• **Selective Breeding**: Developing disease-resistant oyster strains through selective breeding programs can improve the resilience of restored reefs. These strains are bred to tolerate specific pathogens without compromising their ecological functions.

• **Diversified Stocking**: Introducing a mix of oyster species or genetic variants can reduce the risk of disease outbreaks and increase overall reef resilience.

• **Environmental Management**: Adjusting restoration site conditions, such as selecting areas with optimal salinity and temperature ranges, can minimize disease prevalence. For example, cooler, lower-salinity waters are less conducive to many oyster diseases.

Effective disease management requires ongoing research and monitoring to adapt strategies to emerging threats and changing environmental conditions.

Overharvesting

Overharvesting has historically been one of the primary drivers of oyster reef decline. Intensive harvesting practices, such as dredging, have destroyed reef structures, reduced oyster populations, and hindered natural recovery.

1. Impacts on Reefs

The removal of large numbers of oysters disrupts their ability to reproduce and maintain reef structures. Dredging and other destructive harvesting methods damage the physical integrity of reefs, making them more vulnerable to erosion and sedimentation. Overharvesting also depletes the ecosystem services provided by oysters, such as water filtration and habitat creation.

2. Solutions

• **Sustainable Harvesting Practices**: Implementing quotas, size limits, and seasonal closures can prevent overharvesting and allow oyster populations to recover. Encouraging hand-harvesting methods over dredging can reduce physical damage to reefs.

• **Aquaculture Development**: Expanding sustainable oyster farming can relieve pressure on wild populations while providing economic benefits to coastal communities. Farmed oysters can also contribute to water filtration and nutrient cycling, complementing restoration efforts.

• **MPAs**: Designating MPAs or no-take zones where harvesting is prohibited allows oyster reefs to recover and thrive without human interference. These areas serve as reservoirs of biodiversity and sources of larvae for surrounding regions.

Enforcing regulations and raising awareness about the importance of sustainable harvesting are key to preventing further reef degradation.

Integrated Approaches

While pollution, disease, and overharvesting are distinct challenges, they are interconnected and often exacerbate one another. For example, pollution can weaken oysters, making them more susceptible to disease, while overharvesting can reduce reef resilience to environmental stressors. Addressing these challenges requires integrated approaches that consider the broader ecological and socio-economic context of reef restoration.

1. Collaborative Management

Engaging stakeholders, including fishers, policymakers, scientists, and local communities, is essential for effective reef restoration. Collaborative management approaches ensure that restoration efforts are informed by diverse perspectives and address the needs of all stakeholders.

2. Public Awareness and Education

Raising awareness about the ecological and economic value of oyster reefs can foster public support for restoration initiatives. Educational campaigns can encourage sustainable practices and inspire community involvement in restoration efforts, such as shell recycling programs or volunteer-based monitoring.

3. Adaptive Management

Given the dynamic nature of coastal ecosystems, restoration strategies must be flexible and responsive to changing conditions. Adaptive management involves continuous monitoring, evaluation, and adjustment of restoration practices to ensure their long-term success.

Chapter 9: Urban NbS for Coastal Cities

Coastal cities face increasing challenges from climate change, including rising sea levels, storm surges, and erosion. Traditional engineered solutions, such as seawalls and levees, have often been the primary tools for urban resilience, but these approaches can be costly, rigid, and ecologically disruptive. Urban NbS offer an innovative and sustainable alternative, integrating natural processes into city planning and infrastructure to enhance resilience, mitigate risks, and deliver co-benefits like biodiversity support and improved quality of life.

This chapter explores how coastal cities can implement NbS to address their unique vulnerabilities while balancing ecological preservation with urban development. It examines strategies such as green infrastructure, wetland restoration, and the incorporation of living shorelines in urban landscapes. Additionally, the chapter highlights the social, economic, and environmental benefits of urban NbS and discusses the challenges of implementing these solutions in densely populated areas. By understanding the potential of NbS, coastal cities can build more resilient, adaptive, and sustainable futures.

Incorporating Nature-Based Solutions in Urban Areas (Green Roofs, Coastal Parks)

Urban areas, especially in coastal cities, face mounting pressures from climate change, urbanization, and environmental degradation. NbS offer sustainable approaches to mitigate these challenges while enhancing urban resilience and improving quality of life. Two key approaches—green roofs and coastal parks—demonstrate how NbS can be effectively integrated into urban settings to address issues such as flooding, heat mitigation, and biodiversity loss.

Green Roofs

Green roofs, also known as vegetated roofs, involve the installation of soil and plant layers on building rooftops. These systems offer a multifunctional solution to urban challenges, particularly in densely populated coastal cities.

1. Benefits of Green Roofs in Urban NbS

• **Stormwater Management**: Green roofs absorb and store rainwater, reducing surface runoff and alleviating urban flooding. In coastal cities, where heavy rainfall and storm surges exacerbate drainage issues, this function is particularly valuable.

• **Temperature Regulation**: By providing insulation and cooling effects, green roofs mitigate the urban heat island effect, which is often intensified in coastal cities due to dense infrastructure and high humidity.

• **Air Quality Improvement**: Vegetation on green roofs captures particulate matter and pollutants, improving urban air quality.

• **Biodiversity Support**: Green roofs provide habitat for birds, insects, and other species, enhancing biodiversity in urban environments.

2. Types of Green Roofs

• **Extensive Green Roofs**: These are lightweight systems with shallow soil layers, suitable for low-maintenance vegetation like grasses and sedums. They are often used on large rooftops with limited structural capacity.

• **Intensive Green Roofs**: These systems support deeper soil and more diverse plantings, including shrubs and trees, creating rooftop gardens. They require more maintenance but offer greater ecological and aesthetic benefits.

3. Implementation Considerations

Green roof installation requires careful planning to ensure compatibility with building structures and local climate conditions. Factors such as weight capacity, water drainage, and plant selection must be considered to optimize functionality and longevity. Incentive programs, such as subsidies or tax credits, can encourage widespread adoption in urban areas.

Coastal Parks

Coastal parks are another vital component of urban NbS, providing natural buffers against coastal hazards while offering recreational and ecological benefits. These parks often incorporate restored wetlands, dunes, and mangroves to enhance their protective and environmental functions.

1. Benefits of Coastal Parks in Urban NbS

• **Flood Protection**: Coastal parks act as natural flood defenses, absorbing and slowing stormwater and reducing the impact of storm surges on urban areas.

• **Erosion Control**: Features like dunes and vegetation stabilize shorelines, preventing erosion caused by waves and tides.

• **Biodiversity Conservation**: Coastal parks support diverse ecosystems, providing habitats for marine and terrestrial species. In urban areas, these parks reconnect fragmented habitats, promoting ecological balance.

• **Community Well-Being**: Coastal parks offer recreational opportunities, such as walking trails, birdwatching, and water sports, enhancing the quality of life for city residents.

2. Key Design Elements

• **Natural Vegetation**: Incorporating native plants, such as salt-tolerant grasses and shrubs, ensures resilience to coastal conditions and reduces maintenance needs.

• **Water Features**: Restored wetlands and ponds within coastal parks manage stormwater while creating habitats for wildlife.

• **Integrated Infrastructure**: Boardwalks, observation decks, and picnic areas blend recreational spaces with natural environments, fostering community engagement.

3. Implementation Challenges

Creating coastal parks in urban areas often requires overcoming land-use conflicts, high costs, and regulatory barriers. Collaborative planning among government agencies, developers, and local communities is crucial to address these challenges. Public-private partnerships can also play a significant role in funding and maintaining coastal parks.

Integrating Green Roofs and Coastal Parks

The integration of green roofs and coastal parks into urban NbS strategies offers complementary benefits. Green roofs enhance the resilience of individual buildings, while coastal parks provide city-wide protection and recreational spaces. Together, they contribute to a holistic approach to urban sustainability, addressing both localized and systemic challenges.

For example, a coastal city could implement green roofs to manage stormwater and reduce heat in densely developed areas while establishing coastal parks to buffer against flooding and preserve biodiversity. This integrated approach leverages the strengths of both systems, creating a resilient and adaptive urban landscape.

Benefits of Urban Nature-Based Solutions in Managing Stormwater and Heat

Urban NbS are increasingly recognized as essential tools for addressing the dual challenges of stormwater management and urban heat. As cities grow, impervious surfaces such as roads, buildings, and parking lots disrupt natural hydrological cycles and exacerbate heat retention, leading to flooding, water pollution, and the urban heat island effect. NbS, including green infrastructure and restored ecosystems, offer sustainable and multifunctional approaches to mitigate these issues while providing additional ecological, social, and economic benefits.

Managing Stormwater with Urban NbS

Stormwater management is a critical concern in urban areas, where impervious surfaces prevent rainfall from naturally infiltrating the ground. This leads to increased runoff, overwhelmed drainage systems, and urban flooding. Urban NbS help address these issues by mimicking natural hydrological processes to manage, filter, and store stormwater.

1. Green Infrastructure for Stormwater Management

Green infrastructure, such as green roofs, permeable pavements, rain gardens, and bioswales, is a cornerstone of urban NbS for managing stormwater. These systems reduce runoff by capturing and absorbing rainfall, allowing water to infiltrate the soil and replenish groundwater reserves.

• **Green Roofs**: Vegetated rooftops absorb rainwater, reducing the volume and velocity of runoff. They delay peak flows during heavy rain, alleviating pressure on urban drainage systems.

• **Rain Gardens and Bioswales**: These landscaped depressions are designed to capture and filter stormwater. By incorporating native plants, they enhance infiltration and remove pollutants from runoff, improving water quality.

• **Permeable Pavements**: Porous materials allow water to pass through, reducing surface runoff and promoting natural infiltration.

2. Ecosystem Restoration for Flood Mitigation

Restored urban wetlands, riparian zones, and floodplains are highly effective in managing stormwater. These ecosystems act as natural sponges, absorbing excess water and slowly releasing it over time, reducing the risk of flooding.

• **Urban Wetlands**: Rehabilitated wetlands provide storage capacity for stormwater, trapping sediments and pollutants while reducing downstream flooding.

• **Riparian Buffers**: Vegetated corridors along rivers and streams slow runoff and protect waterways from erosion and contamination.

3. Water Quality Improvement

NbS not only manage the volume of stormwater but also improve its quality. Vegetation and soil in green infrastructure systems trap sediments, absorb nutrients, and filter pollutants such as heavy metals and hydrocarbons. This reduces the burden on wastewater treatment facilities and protects aquatic ecosystems.

4. Climate Resilience in Stormwater Management

As climate change intensifies rainfall events, NbS provide adaptive solutions for urban stormwater management. By increasing infiltration, storage capacity, and ecosystem resilience, NbS help cities cope with extreme weather while maintaining ecological integrity.

Mitigating Urban Heat with NbS

The urban heat island (UHI) effect, caused by the concentration of heat-absorbing surfaces and limited vegetation, raises temperatures in cities compared to surrounding rural areas. This phenomenon exacerbates health risks, increases energy demand, and reduces overall urban livability. NbS mitigate the UHI effect by introducing vegetation and water features that cool the urban environment through natural processes.

1. Urban Cooling through Vegetation

Vegetation plays a key role in reducing urban heat through shading and evapotranspiration.

• **Shading**: Trees and plants provide shade, reducing surface and air temperatures. Strategic tree planting along streets, in parks, and near buildings can lower ambient temperatures by several degrees.

• **Evapotranspiration**: Plants release moisture into the air through evapotranspiration, creating a cooling effect. This process is particularly effective in green spaces, where large volumes of vegetation can significantly reduce heat.

2. Green Roofs and Walls

Green roofs and living walls reduce rooftop and façade temperatures, improving building insulation and lowering indoor cooling demands. By replacing heat-absorbing materials with vegetation, these systems reduce the overall heat load in urban areas.

• **Green Roofs**: Vegetation on rooftops cools the surrounding air and reduces heat transfer into buildings. This not only lowers urban temperatures but also decreases energy consumption for air conditioning.

• **Living Walls**: Vertical gardens provide cooling benefits in dense urban environments with limited horizontal space.

3. Blue-Green Infrastructure

NbS that combine vegetation with water features—known as blue-green infrastructure—are highly effective in mitigating heat. Examples include urban wetlands, ponds, and fountains integrated into green spaces.

• **Water Evaporation**: Water features absorb and release heat, cooling the surrounding air through evaporation.

• **Thermal Regulation**: Blue-green systems reduce temperature fluctuations, creating more stable and comfortable urban climates.

4. Urban Parks and Green Corridors

Large urban parks and green corridors act as cooling islands within cities. These spaces provide shade, reduce surface temperatures, and allow for air circulation, dispersing heat from densely built areas.

• **Cooling Zones**: Parks with dense vegetation create localized cooling zones, offering relief during heatwaves.

• **Airflow Enhancement**: Green corridors facilitate the movement of cooler air through cities, reducing overall urban temperatures.

5. Energy Savings and Health Benefits

By reducing urban temperatures, NbS lower energy demand for air conditioning, cutting greenhouse gas emissions and utility costs. Additionally, cooler urban environments improve public health by reducing heat-related illnesses and enhancing overall well-being.

Co-Benefits of Stormwater and Heat Management with NbS

While the primary goals of NbS in urban areas are stormwater and heat management, these solutions also deliver numerous co-benefits.

1. Biodiversity Conservation

Green spaces and restored ecosystems provide habitats for urban wildlife, supporting biodiversity and ecological connectivity.

2. Community Well-Being

Accessible green and blue spaces improve mental and physical health, offering recreational opportunities and fostering social interactions.

3. Economic Resilience

By reducing flooding and cooling costs, NbS contribute to the economic resilience of cities. Well-designed green infrastructure can also attract tourism and investment.

4. Climate Adaptation and Mitigation

NbS enhance urban resilience to climate impacts while sequestering carbon and reducing energy consumption, contributing to global climate goals.

Challenges and Considerations

Despite their benefits, implementing NbS for stormwater and heat management in urban areas presents challenges.

• **Space Constraints**: Densely built cities often lack space for large-scale green infrastructure projects.

• **Cost and Maintenance**: While cost-effective in the long term, initial investment and maintenance costs can be barriers to implementation.

• **Stakeholder Engagement**: Successful NbS projects require collaboration among governments, developers, and local communities to balance competing interests.

Addressing these challenges requires innovative planning, supportive policies, and public-private partnerships to ensure the widespread adoption of NbS.

Integrating Natural and Engineered Solutions in City Planning

The challenges of urbanization, climate change, and environmental degradation have highlighted the need for innovative approaches to urban planning. Integrating natural and engineered solutions offers a balanced pathway to creating resilient, sustainable, and adaptive cities. This hybrid approach combines the ecological benefits of NbS with the reliability and functionality of engineered infrastructure, addressing urban challenges such as flooding, heat mitigation, and resource management while supporting biodiversity and improving quality of life.

Why Integrate Natural and Engineered Solutions?

1. Complementary Strengths

Natural and engineered solutions each bring unique strengths to urban systems. While engineered infrastructure provides immediate and reliable protection against extreme events, natural systems offer adaptability, long-term sustainability, and ecological benefits. By integrating the two, cities can leverage the strengths of both approaches to address complex challenges.

2. Enhanced Resilience

Hybrid solutions improve urban resilience by creating systems that can absorb, adapt to, and recover from environmental stressors. For example, combining stormwater detention basins with restored wetlands can reduce flooding while improving water quality and providing habitat for wildlife.

3. Cost-Effectiveness

Integrating natural elements into engineered systems can reduce costs over time. While engineered infrastructure often requires significant investment and maintenance, natural systems can self-sustain and deliver additional ecosystem services, such as carbon sequestration and recreational opportunities.

Applications of Integrated Solutions in Urban Planning

1. Stormwater Management

Managing stormwater is a critical challenge in urban areas with extensive impervious surfaces. Hybrid solutions combine green infrastructure with traditional drainage systems to mitigate flooding and improve water quality.

• **Bioswales and Underground Drainage**: Bioswales, which are vegetated channels that absorb and filter stormwater, can be paired with underground drainage pipes to handle heavy rainfall events. This combination ensures efficient water management during peak flows while reducing runoff pollution.

• **Retention Ponds and Overflow Systems**: Retention ponds can store excess stormwater and release it gradually, reducing the burden on sewer systems. Incorporating overflow channels ensures that the system can handle extreme events.

2. Coastal Protection

Coastal cities are increasingly vulnerable to sea-level rise and storm surges. Hybrid approaches that integrate natural and engineered solutions provide effective protection while preserving ecological integrity.

• **Living Shorelines with Breakwaters**: Living shorelines, which use vegetation and natural materials, can be combined with engineered breakwaters to reduce wave energy and prevent erosion. Breakwaters provide immediate protection, while living shorelines offer long-term adaptability and ecological benefits.

• **Mangrove Planting with Seawalls**: In tropical regions, mangroves can be planted in front of seawalls to absorb wave energy and trap sediments. The mangroves enhance biodiversity and carbon sequestration, while the seawalls provide robust protection against extreme events.

3. Urban Heat Mitigation

The urban heat island effect poses significant risks to public health and energy systems. Hybrid solutions integrate natural cooling elements into urban infrastructure to reduce temperatures and improve comfort.

• **Green Roofs and Insulation**: Green roofs reduce rooftop temperatures through evapotranspiration, while engineered insulation enhances building energy efficiency. Together, these systems reduce cooling costs and indoor heat exposure.

• **Urban Parks with Cooling Technology**: Large parks with dense vegetation provide natural cooling through shade and evapotranspiration. Installing misting systems or fountains within these parks amplifies the cooling effect, offering relief during heatwaves.

4. Transportation Networks

Hybrid solutions can make urban transportation networks more sustainable and climate-resilient.

• **Permeable Pavements with Subsurface Drainage**: Permeable pavements allow water infiltration, reducing runoff. Combining these with subsurface drainage systems ensures that roads remain functional during heavy rainfall.

• **Green Corridors with Elevated Infrastructure**: Green corridors with integrated pedestrian and cycling paths can be paired with elevated rail systems. This dual-purpose infrastructure reduces emissions, supports active transportation, and enhances biodiversity.

Benefits of Integration

1. Multifunctionality

Hybrid systems provide multiple benefits, addressing infrastructure needs while enhancing ecological functions. For instance, a flood detention basin with wetland features not only manages stormwater but also supports biodiversity, improves water quality, and offers recreational opportunities.

2. Long-Term Sustainability

Natural systems adapt to changing conditions, such as rising sea levels or increased rainfall, reducing the need for frequent infrastructure upgrades. When paired with engineered systems, they create durable solutions that require less intervention over time.

3. Social and Economic Value

Integrated solutions contribute to urban livability by creating green spaces, improving air and water quality, and reducing disaster risks. These benefits enhance public well-being and attract investment, boosting local economies.

4. Climate Adaptation

Hybrid approaches are particularly effective in addressing climate impacts. By combining the robustness of engineered systems with the adaptability of natural systems, cities can better cope with extreme weather, rising temperatures, and changing environmental conditions.

Challenges and Solutions

1. Complexity in Design and Implementation

Integrating natural and engineered solutions requires multidisciplinary expertise and collaboration among planners, engineers, and ecologists. To address this, cities can invest in capacity-building and foster partnerships between stakeholders.

2. Maintenance Requirements

While natural systems often require less maintenance over time, hybrid systems may still need regular upkeep. Clear maintenance plans and community involvement can ensure the longevity of these solutions.

3. Land Availability

Urban areas often face space constraints, making it challenging to implement large-scale natural systems. Innovative designs, such as vertical green walls or rooftop wetlands, can maximize the use of limited space.

Chapter 10: Scaling Up NbS for Global Coastal Restoration

As the impacts of climate change intensify and coastal ecosystems face unprecedented threats, scaling up NbS has become a global priority for restoring and protecting coastal environments. From mitigating erosion and enhancing biodiversity to safeguarding communities from storm surges and sea-level rise, NbS offer sustainable, adaptable, and cost-effective approaches to address complex coastal challenges. However, implementing these solutions on a global scale requires overcoming barriers related to funding, governance, capacity building, and stakeholder engagement.

This chapter explores strategies for scaling up NbS for coastal restoration, focusing on policy frameworks, international collaborations, and technological innovations that can drive widespread adoption. It emphasizes the importance of integrating NbS into global climate and development agendas, ensuring equitable benefits for vulnerable communities, and fostering knowledge sharing across regions. By examining pathways for expansion, this chapter highlights how scaling up NbS can create resilient coastal ecosystems and contribute to a sustainable future.

Importance of Scaling Nature-Based Solutions Globally

Scaling NbS globally is vital to addressing the growing environmental, social, and economic challenges posed by climate change, biodiversity loss, and coastal degradation. As coastal ecosystems face escalating pressures, from rising sea levels and severe storms to pollution and habitat destruction, NbS offer an integrated approach to restore ecosystems, protect communities, and enhance resilience. By implementing these solutions at a global scale, nations can collectively respond to these challenges while advancing sustainable development and climate adaptation goals.

Addressing Global Environmental Challenges

1. Climate Change Mitigation and Adaptation

Coastal ecosystems, such as mangroves, seagrass meadows, and salt marshes, play a critical role in mitigating climate change by sequestering significant amounts of carbon. Scaling NbS globally enhances the capacity of these ecosystems to act as carbon sinks, reducing greenhouse gas concentrations.

Moreover, NbS help communities adapt to climate impacts by protecting coastlines from erosion, storm surges, and sea-level rise. For example, restoring mangroves reduces wave energy and provides a natural buffer against extreme weather events, safeguarding both ecosystems and infrastructure.

2. Biodiversity Conservation

The global decline in biodiversity is particularly pronounced in coastal and marine environments, where habitat loss and degradation are widespread. Scaling up NbS contributes to restoring critical habitats, such as coral reefs and wetlands, which support a diverse range of species. By enhancing ecological connectivity and protecting natural systems, NbS help maintain biodiversity and ecosystem functionality at a regional and global scale.

3. Water Quality Improvement

Global-scale NbS initiatives improve water quality in coastal regions by filtering pollutants and reducing sedimentation. Wetlands and oyster reefs, for instance, remove excess nutrients and contaminants from water, mitigating the impacts of agricultural runoff and urban wastewater. Scaling these solutions ensures healthier coastal waters, supporting fisheries, tourism, and public health.

Promoting Social and Economic Resilience

1. Protecting Vulnerable Communities

Many of the world's most vulnerable populations live in low-lying coastal areas that are highly susceptible to climate-related hazards. Scaling NbS provides these communities with natural defenses against flooding and storms, reducing economic losses and enhancing safety. In addition, NbS support sustainable livelihoods by bolstering fisheries, eco-tourism, and agriculture.

2. Economic Benefits and Cost-Effectiveness

Compared to traditional infrastructure, NbS are often more cost-effective over the long term. Natural systems can self-sustain and adapt to environmental changes, reducing maintenance costs. Scaling NbS globally promotes economic resilience by minimizing disaster recovery expenses and creating jobs in restoration, monitoring, and eco-tourism.

3. Health and Well-Being

Expanding NbS improves public health by enhancing air and water quality, reducing heat stress in urban coastal areas, and providing green spaces for recreation. These benefits are particularly critical in densely populated coastal cities, where environmental degradation directly affects residents' quality of life.

Advancing Global Policy and Development Goals

1. Aligning with International Frameworks

Scaling NbS aligns with major international frameworks, including the Paris Agreement, the United Nations SDGs, and the Convention on Biological Diversity (CBD). NbS contribute to achieving climate targets, ensuring sustainable use of marine resources, and protecting biodiversity. By integrating NbS into national and international policies, governments can address multiple objectives simultaneously.

2. Cross-Border Collaboration

Coastal ecosystems often span national boundaries, making international cooperation essential for effective restoration. Scaling NbS facilitates cross-border collaborations that promote shared knowledge, resources, and technology. For example, multinational initiatives to restore coral reefs or protect migratory species ensure coordinated efforts across regions.

3. Long-Term Sustainability

Global-scale NbS initiatives emphasize long-term sustainability by prioritizing community involvement, equitable resource distribution, and adaptive management. These principles ensure that solutions are resilient to future challenges and benefit diverse stakeholders, including marginalized communities disproportionately affected by climate change.

Overcoming Barriers to Global Implementation

While the benefits of scaling NbS are clear, achieving global implementation requires addressing key barriers. Limited funding, governance challenges, and lack of technical capacity can hinder widespread adoption. Collaborative efforts among governments, non-governmental organizations, the private sector, and local communities are critical to overcoming these obstacles.

1. Financing NbS

Scaling NbS globally demands innovative financing mechanisms, such as public-private partnerships, green bonds, and international climate funds. These approaches ensure sustained investment in restoration projects and enable broader participation in global initiatives.

2. Capacity Building and Knowledge Sharing

Expanding NbS at scale requires technical expertise and robust data to inform planning and implementation. Global platforms for knowledge exchange, training programs, and research collaborations can build capacity across regions, ensuring that lessons learned are widely disseminated.

3. Policy Integration and Stakeholder Engagement

Embedding NbS into national and regional policies ensures institutional support for scaling efforts. Engaging stakeholders, including local communities, ensures that NbS are culturally appropriate and meet the needs of those most affected by coastal challenges.

Strategies for Replication and Adaptation in Diverse Ecosystems

The successful replication and adaptation of NbS across diverse ecosystems are essential for scaling global coastal restoration efforts. Every coastal environment—be it tropical mangroves, temperate salt marshes, or coral reefs—presents unique challenges and opportunities. Strategies for replication and adaptation must consider ecological, social, and economic differences to ensure that NbS are both effective and sustainable. By tailoring approaches to specific environmental contexts while maintaining core principles, NbS can be applied successfully in a wide range of ecosystems.

1. Core Principles of Replication and Adaptation

To replicate and adapt NbS effectively, it is essential to adhere to the following principles:

• **Ecosystem-Specific Design**: NbS must be tailored to the ecological characteristics of the target ecosystem, including its biodiversity, hydrology, and geomorphology.

• **Community Involvement**: Local communities should be engaged throughout the planning and implementation process to ensure solutions align with cultural, social, and economic priorities.

• **Scalability and Flexibility**: NbS should be designed to scale and adapt to changing conditions, such as climate impacts or urban expansion.

• **Monitoring and Feedback**: Continuous monitoring and feedback mechanisms are necessary to assess effectiveness and make adjustments as needed.

2. Strategies for Tropical Ecosystems

a. Mangroves

Mangroves play a critical role in tropical coastal ecosystems, providing protection against storm surges, supporting fisheries, and sequestering carbon. Replication strategies for mangrove restoration focus on addressing site-specific factors such as salinity, tidal patterns, and sediment availability.

• **Site Selection and Preparation**: Identify degraded mangrove areas with suitable hydrological conditions. Remove barriers to natural tidal flow, such as dykes or channels, to facilitate natural regeneration.

• **Community Engagement**: Collaborate with local communities to ensure sustainable use of mangrove resources. Community-led replanting programs using native species can enhance long-term success.

• **Adaptive Planting Techniques**: Use techniques such as cluster planting and propagule anchoring to stabilize sediments and promote natural regeneration.

b. Coral Reefs

Coral reefs in tropical regions face threats from warming seas, ocean acidification, and overfishing. Replication strategies focus on restoring coral health and enhancing resilience.

• **Coral Gardening**: Grow coral fragments in underwater nurseries and transplant them to degraded reefs.

• **Genetic Diversity**: Use resilient coral strains to enhance the reef's ability to withstand environmental stressors.

• **Integrated Protection**: Combine reef restoration with measures such as marine protected areas and sustainable fishing practices.

3. Strategies for Temperate Ecosystems

a. Salt Marshes

Salt marshes provide critical ecosystem services, including flood mitigation, water filtration, and habitat provision. In temperate zones, strategies for salt marsh restoration prioritize sediment dynamics and vegetation establishment.

• **Sediment Augmentation**: Use dredged material or natural sediment flows to rebuild marsh elevation and combat sea-level rise.

• **Planting Native Vegetation**: Introduce salt-tolerant plants, such as *Spartina alterniflora*, to stabilize sediments and promote natural expansion.

• **Hydrological Restoration**: Reestablish tidal flows by removing barriers such as levees or drainage ditches.

b. Oyster Reefs

Temperate coastal waters are ideal for oyster reef restoration, which enhances biodiversity, filters water, and stabilizes shorelines.

• **Spat-on-Shell Techniques**: Use hatchery-reared larvae attached to shells for large-scale reef restoration.

• **Hybrid Structures**: Combine natural oyster reefs with artificial substrates, such as reef balls or breakwaters, to enhance stability in high-energy environments.

• **Water Quality Monitoring**: Ensure that restoration sites have optimal salinity and minimal pollution to support oyster survival and growth.

4. Strategies for Urban Coastal Areas

Urban coastal environments pose unique challenges due to space constraints, pollution, and intense human activity. Strategies for replicating NbS in these areas emphasize integration with urban infrastructure.

a. Green Infrastructure

Green roofs, rain gardens, and bioswales can manage stormwater while enhancing biodiversity in urban settings.

• **Customizable Designs**: Adapt green infrastructure to available space, such as rooftops, parking lots, and urban parks.

• **Community Education**: Engage residents in maintaining green spaces and promoting awareness of their benefits.

b. Living Shorelines

Living shorelines, which integrate vegetation, reefs, and other natural elements, can be adapted to urban environments.

• **Modular Solutions**: Use modular designs, such as pre-planted coir mats, to fit living shorelines into constrained urban spaces.

• **Combined Engineering**: Pair living shorelines with seawalls or bulkheads to enhance protection in densely populated areas.

5. Strategies for Cold and Polar Regions

Cold and polar regions face unique challenges due to extreme weather, ice dynamics, and limited biodiversity. NbS in these areas often focus on enhancing natural resilience to protect coastal systems.

a. Arctic Wetlands

Wetlands in polar regions provide critical carbon storage and flood regulation.

• **Permafrost Stabilization**: Protect permafrost by restoring wetland vegetation, which insulates the ground and reduces thawing.

• **Hydrological Management**: Ensure natural water flow is maintained to support wetland ecosystems.

b. Kelp Forests

Kelp forests in cold waters support marine biodiversity and absorb carbon.

• **Replanting Efforts**: Use kelp farming techniques to reestablish degraded forests.

• **Nutrient Management**: Reduce nutrient pollution to prevent harmful algal blooms that compete with kelp.

6. Cross-Cutting Strategies

Certain strategies apply across diverse ecosystems, enhancing replication and adaptation efforts globally:

• **Technology and Innovation**: Use remote sensing, GIS, and modeling tools to identify restoration sites and monitor progress.

• **Policy Integration**: Incorporate NbS into national and regional policies, ensuring long-term support and funding.

• **Capacity Building**: Provide training for local stakeholders and practitioners to implement and maintain NbS effectively.

• **Knowledge Sharing**: Establish global networks to exchange best practices and lessons learned across regions.

Future Directions and Partnerships for Scaling Nature-Based Solutions

The successful implementation and scaling of NbS for coastal restoration depend on forward-looking strategies and robust partnerships. As climate change intensifies and coastal ecosystems face mounting pressures, governments, organizations, and communities must collaborate to drive innovation, secure funding, and create enabling environments for NbS. Future efforts will focus on expanding research, fostering cross-sectoral partnerships, and integrating NbS into global and local policy frameworks. This section outlines key future directions and the importance of partnerships in advancing the global NbS agenda.

Future Directions for Scaling NbS

1. Advancing Scientific Research and Technology

To enhance the effectiveness and scalability of NbS, future efforts must prioritize scientific research and the application of cutting-edge technology.

• **Monitoring and Modeling**: Improved monitoring tools, such as remote sensing and GIS, will help track the performance of NbS projects and optimize their design. Predictive models can simulate long-term outcomes, informing adaptive management strategies.

• **Innovative Techniques**: Research into resilient species, hybrid solutions, and bioengineering techniques will expand the scope of NbS in diverse environments. For example, developing heat-tolerant coral strains or high-yield mangrove propagules can enhance restoration in challenging conditions.

• **Data Sharing Platforms**: Establishing global databases of NbS case studies and outcomes will facilitate knowledge exchange and inspire replication across regions.

2. Policy Integration and Incentives

Embedding NbS into policy frameworks is essential to ensure their widespread adoption and funding.

• **Global Commitments**: Incorporating NbS into international agreements, such as the Paris Agreement and the United Nations SDGs, will provide a foundation for coordinated action.

• **National and Local Policies**: Governments can incentivize NbS through policies that support green infrastructure, community-led restoration, and ecosystem-based adaptation. Tax credits, grants, and subsidies for NbS projects can encourage private sector participation.

- **Regulatory Alignment**: Harmonizing policies across sectors, such as coastal management, agriculture, and urban planning, will create synergies that amplify the benefits of NbS.

3. Climate Adaptation and Mitigation Synergies

Future NbS initiatives must address both climate adaptation and mitigation goals.

- **Carbon Sequestration**: Coastal ecosystems, such as mangroves and seagrass meadows, play a vital role in capturing and storing carbon. Scaling these systems can contribute significantly to global emissions reduction targets.

- **Risk Reduction**: NbS will be central to reducing climate-related risks, such as storm surges and sea-level rise, by enhancing the resilience of coastal infrastructure and communities.

4. Community Empowerment and Equity

Ensuring that NbS projects are inclusive and equitable will be critical for their long-term success.

- **Local Involvement**: Engaging local communities in planning, implementation, and monitoring ensures that NbS address specific needs and priorities.

- **Equitable Benefits**: Restoration projects must consider vulnerable populations, ensuring that the benefits of NbS, such as improved livelihoods and reduced climate risks, are distributed fairly.

- **Capacity Building**: Providing training and resources to local stakeholders will empower them to lead NbS efforts and sustain their outcomes.

Partnerships to Drive NbS Expansion

Scaling NbS globally requires collaboration across sectors, borders, and disciplines. Partnerships will play a pivotal role in pooling resources, expertise, and political will to advance NbS initiatives.

1. Public-Private Partnerships (PPPs)

Collaboration between governments and the private sector can unlock funding and technical expertise for large-scale NbS projects.

• **Corporate Investment**: Companies can invest in NbS as part of their corporate social responsibility (CSR) or sustainability initiatives. For example, coastal restoration projects can align with carbon offset goals.

• **Co-Financing Models**: PPPs can share costs and risks, ensuring that projects are financially viable and deliver long-term benefits.

2. International and Regional Cooperation

Global and regional partnerships can facilitate knowledge sharing, resource mobilization, and coordinated action.

• **Multilateral Organizations**: Institutions like the United Nations, World Bank, and Global Environment Facility (GEF) provide financial and technical support for NbS initiatives.

• **Regional Alliances**: Cross-border collaborations, such as the Coral Triangle Initiative or the European Green Deal, promote coordinated restoration efforts in shared ecosystems.

3. Academic and Research Collaborations

Partnerships between universities, research institutions, and conservation organizations are vital for advancing NbS science and practice.

• **Interdisciplinary Research**: Collaborative research efforts can explore the ecological, social, and economic dimensions of NbS, generating holistic solutions.

• **Educational Programs**: Universities can develop specialized training programs to equip the next generation of NbS practitioners with the skills needed for implementation and scaling.

4. Community-Led Partnerships

Empowering local communities through partnerships ensures that NbS are contextually relevant and sustainable.

• **Non-Governmental Organizations (NGOs)**: NGOs can bridge the gap between local communities and large institutions, providing technical support and advocacy for community-driven restoration projects.

• **Citizen Science**: Engaging citizens in monitoring and data collection fosters stewardship and enhances public understanding of NbS benefits.

Overcoming Barriers Through Collaboration

Despite the potential of NbS, scaling them globally requires addressing key challenges, including funding gaps, governance complexities, and technical constraints. Collaborative efforts can help overcome these barriers:

• **Innovative Financing**: Establishing green bonds, climate funds, and PES schemes can generate sustainable financing for NbS.

• **Policy Cohesion**: Partnerships between policymakers, scientists, and industry leaders can ensure that regulatory frameworks support NbS.

• **Capacity Building**: Joint training programs and knowledge exchanges can equip stakeholders with the tools to implement and maintain NbS effectively.

Conclusion

The global imperative to restore and protect coastal ecosystems has never been more urgent. NbS offer a transformative approach to addressing the complex challenges posed by climate change, biodiversity loss, and coastal degradation. This book has explored the diverse types of NbS, their ecological and social benefits, and the strategies for scaling their implementation globally.

In this concluding chapter, we synthesize the key insights from the preceding chapters, emphasizing the importance of adopting a holistic and inclusive approach to coastal restoration. We reflect on the progress made, identify the remaining gaps, and outline actionable recommendations for advancing NbS. By fostering partnerships, integrating NbS into policy frameworks, and leveraging innovation, the global community can create resilient and sustainable coastal ecosystems that support both nature and people. This chapter aims to inspire continued action and collaboration to ensure a thriving future for our coastal environments.

Summary of Nature-Based Solutions Types and Their Benefits

NbS encompass a wide range of approaches designed to address environmental, social, and economic challenges by leveraging natural processes. In the context of coastal restoration, these solutions aim to restore ecosystems, enhance resilience, and provide sustainable benefits to communities and biodiversity. This summary highlights the primary types of NbS discussed and their key benefits.

1. Mangroves

Mangroves are vital coastal ecosystems that provide protection, biodiversity, and carbon sequestration. These salt-tolerant trees and shrubs grow along tropical and subtropical coastlines, offering multiple benefits:

• **Coastal Protection**: Mangroves reduce wave energy and storm surges, minimizing coastal erosion and safeguarding infrastructure.

• **Biodiversity Support**: They serve as nurseries for fish, crustaceans, and other marine life, supporting fisheries and ecosystem health.

• **Carbon Sequestration**: Mangroves store significant amounts of carbon in their biomass and soils, contributing to climate change mitigation.

2. Coral Reefs

Coral reefs are critical for marine biodiversity and coastal protection, particularly in tropical regions. They provide essential ecosystem services:

• **Wave Energy Dissipation**: Coral reefs act as natural breakwaters, reducing the impact of waves and protecting coastlines from erosion.

• **Habitat Creation**: These ecosystems support a vast array of marine species, promoting biodiversity and fisheries productivity.

• **Tourism and Recreation**: Healthy coral reefs attract tourists, generating income for coastal communities.

3. Seagrass Meadows

Seagrass meadows are submerged aquatic habitats that play a key role in maintaining healthy coastal ecosystems:

• **Carbon Storage**: Seagrasses sequester carbon in their biomass and sediments, aiding in climate mitigation.

• **Water Quality Improvement**: They filter pollutants and trap sediments, enhancing water clarity and quality.

• **Biodiversity**: Seagrass meadows provide food and shelter for a variety of marine organisms, including fish, turtles, and invertebrates.

4. Salt Marshes

Salt marshes are intertidal wetlands dominated by salt-tolerant vegetation. They deliver numerous benefits for coastal areas:

• **Flood Mitigation**: By absorbing stormwater and slowing floodwaters, salt marshes reduce the risk of coastal flooding.

• **Erosion Control**: The root systems of marsh vegetation stabilize sediments, preventing shoreline erosion.

• **Wildlife Habitat**: Salt marshes provide critical habitats for birds, fish, and invertebrates, supporting ecological diversity.

5. Oyster and Shellfish Reefs

Oyster and shellfish reefs offer both ecological and protective benefits to coastal communities:

• **Wave Attenuation**: These reefs act as natural barriers, reducing wave energy and protecting shorelines.

• **Water Filtration**: Oysters filter large volumes of water, improving water quality and reducing nutrient pollution.

• **Biodiversity Hotspots**: Reefs provide habitats for fish, crabs, and other marine life, enhancing ecosystem productivity.

6. Living Shorelines

Living shorelines integrate natural elements like vegetation and oyster reefs with low-impact engineering to stabilize coastlines:

• **Erosion Reduction**: Vegetation and reefs dissipate wave energy, preventing erosion and shoreline loss.

• **Habitat Support**: These systems create habitats for coastal and marine species.

• **Resilience**: Living shorelines adapt to changing conditions, such as rising sea levels, providing sustainable protection.

7. Urban NbS

In urban coastal areas, NbS include green roofs, coastal parks, and blue-green infrastructure. These solutions offer unique benefits in densely populated environments:

• **Stormwater Management**: Green roofs and rain gardens absorb and filter rainwater, reducing urban flooding.

• **Heat Mitigation**: Vegetation and water features lower urban temperatures, combating the heat island effect.

• **Recreational Opportunities**: Coastal parks and green spaces improve community well-being and provide aesthetic value.

Cumulative Benefits of NbS

Across these types, NbS share common benefits that contribute to global sustainability goals:

- **Ecosystem Restoration**: NbS restore degraded habitats, enhancing biodiversity and ecological resilience.

- **Climate Adaptation and Mitigation**: They protect against climate impacts while sequestering carbon.

- **Economic Value**: By supporting fisheries, tourism, and ecosystem services, NbS generate economic benefits for communities.

- **Social and Cultural Benefits**: NbS improve quality of life by providing recreational spaces, protecting livelihoods, and fostering a connection to nature.

Lessons Learned and Actionable Recommendations

The implementation of NbS for coastal restoration has provided valuable insights into their potential, challenges, and strategies for success. Reflecting on these lessons allows for refining approaches and offering actionable recommendations to scale NbS globally. This section highlights key takeaways and practical steps for advancing NbS initiatives.

Lessons Learned

1. Ecosystem-Specific Design is Crucial

NbS must be tailored to the unique characteristics of each coastal ecosystem. Factors such as hydrology, biodiversity, and local climate conditions influence the success of restoration efforts. Generic solutions often fail to address specific ecological or social needs, emphasizing the importance of customized designs.

2. Community Involvement Enhances Success

Engaging local communities from the planning stage through implementation ensures that NbS align with their needs and priorities. Community participation fosters a sense of ownership, which is critical for the long-term sustainability of projects. Successful examples demonstrate the importance of integrating traditional ecological knowledge with modern practices.

3. Policy and Funding Are Key Enablers

Strong policy support and sustainable funding mechanisms are essential for scaling NbS. Many projects face challenges due to fragmented governance or limited resources. Aligning NbS initiatives with national and international frameworks, such as the Paris Agreement or SDGs, can unlock funding and institutional support.

4. Monitoring and Adaptive Management Drive Longevity

Continuous monitoring and adaptive management are necessary to ensure that NbS remain effective over time. Changing environmental conditions, such as rising sea levels or temperature fluctuations, require flexible approaches. Data-driven decision-making helps refine practices and address emerging challenges.

5. Partnerships Strengthen Implementation

Collaboration among governments, NGOs, the private sector, and research institutions is crucial for pooling resources, expertise, and innovation. Partnerships enable larger-scale and more impactful projects, particularly in transboundary ecosystems.

Actionable Recommendations

1. Scale Up Community-Led Projects

• Empower local stakeholders by providing technical training and financial support.

• Promote citizen science initiatives to involve communities in monitoring and maintaining NbS.

• Ensure that projects address equity concerns, prioritizing the needs of vulnerable populations.

2. Foster Policy Integration

• Embed NbS into national climate adaptation and mitigation strategies.

• Develop regulatory incentives, such as tax benefits or grants, to encourage private sector participation.

• Create cross-sectoral policies that link NbS with urban planning, agriculture, and disaster management.

3. Secure Innovative Financing

• Establish funding mechanisms like green bonds, payment-for-ecosystem-services schemes, and public-private partnerships.

• Leverage international climate funds, such as the Green Climate Fund, to support large-scale NbS initiatives.

4. Invest in Research and Technology

• Advance research on resilient species and innovative restoration techniques.

• Use technology, such as remote sensing and GIS, for site assessment, monitoring, and scaling projects.

• Share knowledge through global databases and collaborative platforms.

5. Prioritize Education and Awareness

• Raise public awareness about the benefits of NbS through campaigns and educational programs.

• Incorporate NbS topics into academic curricula to train the next generation of practitioners.

Vision for the Future of Coastal Ecosystems

The future of coastal ecosystems holds immense potential if humanity embraces sustainable practices and prioritizes the restoration and preservation of these critical environments. Coastal ecosystems, such as mangroves, coral reefs, seagrass meadows, and salt marshes, serve as vital buffers against climate impacts, support biodiversity, and provide invaluable services to human communities. A forward-looking vision for these ecosystems recognizes their ecological importance and underscores the need for proactive, inclusive, and innovative solutions.

A Resilient and Restored Coastal Environment

The future envisions coastal ecosystems as thriving, resilient systems capable of adapting to climate change and human pressures. NbS will play a central role in restoring degraded ecosystems, enhancing biodiversity, and mitigating risks from sea-level rise, storm surges, and coastal erosion. Through targeted restoration efforts, ecosystems will recover their natural functionality, ensuring they continue to provide essential services such as carbon sequestration, water filtration, and fisheries support.

Integration with Human Systems

A sustainable future for coastal ecosystems also envisions their seamless integration with urban and rural human systems. Coastal cities and communities will adopt hybrid approaches that combine natural processes with engineered infrastructure to address challenges such as flooding and heat stress. Living shorelines, green infrastructure, and blue-green corridors will become standard components of urban planning, balancing human development with ecosystem preservation.

Global Collaboration and Local Empowerment

Achieving this vision requires a global commitment to collaboration and local empowerment. Governments, international organizations, and NGOs will work together to establish transboundary conservation initiatives, ensuring the protection of ecosystems that span multiple countries. Simultaneously, local communities will be at the forefront of restoration efforts, supported by funding, training, and resources that enable them to sustain these projects over time.

Education, Innovation, and Equity

Education and technological innovation will drive progress in coastal conservation. Research into climate-resilient species, advanced restoration techniques, and data-driven monitoring will enhance the effectiveness of NbS. Public awareness campaigns and educational programs will cultivate a global understanding of the value of coastal ecosystems. Importantly, efforts will prioritize equity, ensuring that vulnerable populations benefit from restoration initiatives and that resources are distributed fairly.

Conclusion

The vision for the future of coastal ecosystems is one of resilience, integration, and equity. By embracing sustainable practices and innovative solutions, humanity can ensure that these ecosystems continue to thrive, providing critical benefits for both nature and people in the face of evolving challenges.

www.ingramcontent.com/pod-product-compliance
Lightning Source LLC
Chambersburg PA
CBHW052135270326
41930CB00012B/2902